The Beatitudes in Context
What Luke and Matthew Meant

Zacchaeus Studies: New Testament

General Editor: Mary Ann Getty, RSM

The Beatitudes in Context
What Luke and Matthew Meant

by

M. Dennis Hamm, S.J.

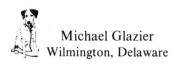

Michael Glazier
Wilmington, Delaware

First published in 1990 by Michael Glazier, Inc., 1935 West Fourth Street, Wilmington, Delaware 19805.

Library of Congress Cataloging-in-Publication Data

Hamm, M. Dennis.
   THE BEATITUDES IN CONTEXT; WHAT LUKE AND MATTHEW MEANT / by M. Dennis Hamm.
      p. cm. — (Zacchaeus studies. New Testament)
   Includes bibliographical references.
   ISBN 0-89453-676-1

   1. Beatitudes—Criticism, interpretation, etc. I. Title.
II. Series.
BT382.H226   1989
226'.9306—dc20

89-39265
CIP

Cover Design by Maureen Daney
Typography by Cyndi Cohee
Printed in the United States by St. Mary's

Table of Contents

Editor's Note vii

Introduction 1

Part One: Some Preliminary Questions

I. What's a Macarism? 7
II. What Does a Macarism Do? 11
III. A First Reading: Questioning the Texts 13
IV. A Version Behind the Versions?
    The "Q" Beatitudes 16
V. The Beatitudes' Meaning in Jesus' Ministry 20

Part Two: The Beatitudes (and Woes)
According to Luke

I. Who Is Talking? 27
II. To Whom is He Talking? 37
III. What Time Is It? 41
IV. Who Are the Poor and the Rich in
    Luke's Beatitudes and Woes? 44
V. What Is Jesus Saying? 57
VI. Confirmations and Clarifications
    from Luke's Narrative 61

Part Three: The Beatitudes of Matthew

I. Preliminaries: Who Speaks to Whom, When? 69
II. The Message of the Matthean Jesus 79

Afterword 110
Suggested Readings 115
Indices 117

*For my parents
Agnes and Victor
whose lives and work
have taught me the love
of words and the Word*

Editor's Note

Zacchaeus Studies provide concise, readable and relatively inexpensive scholarly studies on particular aspects of scripture and theology. The New Testament section of the series presents studies dealing with focal or debated questions; and the volumes focus on specific texts of particular themes of current interest in biblical interpretation. Specialists have their professional journals and other forums where they discuss matters of mutual concern, exchange ideas and further contemporary trends of research; and some of their work on contemporary biblical research is now made accessible for students and others in *Zacchaeus Studies.*

The authors in this series share their own scholarship in non-technical language, in the areas of their expertise and interest. These writers stand with the best in current biblical scholarship in the English-speaking world. Since most of them are teachers, they are accustomed to presenting difficult material in comprehensible form without compromising a high level of critical judgment and analysis.

The works of this series are ecumenical in content and purpose and cross credal boundaries. They are designed to augment formal and informal biblical study and discussion. Hopefully they will also serve as texts to enhance and supplement seminary, university and college classes. The series will also aid Bible study groups, adult education and parish religious education classes to develop intelligent, versatile and challenging programs for those they serve.

Mary Ann Getty RSM
New Testament Editor

Introduction

In our religious imaginations, the beatitudes have often lived a kind of disembodied life of their own. Printed separately in prayer books, chiseled into marble, stitched onto banners, they sometimes work in our minds like a Rorschach inkblot onto which we project our own hopes and fears. At other times, they tease us like a series of zen koans (sample koan: "What is the sound of one hand clapping?"). In fact, beatitudes are nothing of the sort. The Rorschach inkblot is meant to be an empty form which draws out some of the contents of our subconscious mind. A koan is designed to tease the mind beyond conventional modes of thinking and thereby to empty the mind. A beatitude, on the other hand, is a conventional literary form with a long tradition, whose purpose has always been to communicate with clarity and power. As always when Jesus uses the traditional literary forms of his people, he uses the beatitude form with a keen sense of the convention and with startling originality. We are in danger of misunderstanding Jesus if we listen to his beatitudes apart from their natural environment of the Hebrew Scriptures and if we cut them from their gospel contexts.

Luke 11:27-28 presents Jesus trading beatitudes with a woman in the crowd. She says, "Blessed is the womb that bore you and the breasts that nursed you"—which is obviously not a physiological observation but a praising of the mother of such a son (as well as an indirect compliment to the son). Jesus answers with a beatitude of his own: it is not simply for her maternal relationship that Mary is to be congratulated but even more for her faithfulness to God. He says, "Rather blessed are they who hear the word of God and keep it."

This exchange begins to catch the flavor of the sayings which we usually think of as the beatitudes, those at the head of the famous Sermon. Nothing could be more conventional than a woman congratulating another woman on the quality of her offspring. But Jesus chooses to confront this beatitude with another, in order to assert a religious truth. Being a faithful daughter of God is greater than being a successful mother, even when these qualities appear in the same person. But even here, once the woman had gulped down the impact of the confrontation, she would have recognized the traditional Jewish wisdom contained in Jesus' response.

In the beatitudes that introduce the Sermon on the Mount, however, the voltage of confrontation makes a quantum leap. "Blessed are the poor; for the reign of God is yours." That flies in the face of conventional wisdom. Everyday experience does not seem to support it. "Blessed are you who hunger now; you shall be filled." This seems, on the face of it, to be wishful thinking. "Blessed are the meek; they shall inherit the land." Why, then, is land reform in Latin America such a bloody business?

The more seriously the contemporary reader takes the beatitudes of Jesus, the more questions they raise. Matthew has "poor *in spirit*" where Luke simply has "poor." Which is more likely to be closer to the words of Jesus? Does Matthew water down the word of the Master? Or does Luke change it, simplifying the original? In what sense, and at what time (this life, or the next?) do the poor actually possess the kingdom of God? Can a pastor be content to tell the poorer members of the flock that things will be better after they die?

And what is "purity of heart"? Does that purity have something to do with sex? What is the connection between that purity and seeing God? Some translators prefer "holiness" to "justice" in the saying "Blessed are those who are persecuted for justice's sake." Does that mean the eighth beatitude bears no relationship to the contemporary struggle for social justice, say, in the Philippines, in South Africa, or in the United States?

The questions are many. Yet for all their confrontational, mind-teasing qualities, the beatitudes of Jesus are not zen koans. They are not expressions of a tradition which aims at evacuating the mind of imaginative content. Biblical writing is not zen discipline. Biblical language, in any and all of its many literary forms, speaks *to* and *through* but not *past* the human imagination. Biblical imagery is meant to be listened to carefully and taken seriously. There is no other way to listen to the revelation which is Scripture. The vehicle of divine revelation is the homey imagery of human language. And the beatitudes of Jesus are, in this respect, no exception. They are expressed in language deeply rooted in the biblical tradition. Moreover, they are integrated, with great care and skill, into the literary fabric of their respective gospels.

It is this realization which encourages me to venture into a field already so thoroughly worked over. The exegetical, homiletic, and devotional literature on the beatitudes is vast. [1] The investigation of the OT background is also extensive.[2] But there is an approach to the study of the beatitudes which has only begun to be fully explored in our own generation. I am referring to the insight which emerges when one takes seriously the *literary context* of the beatitudes. The techniques of redaction criticism and composition criticism boldly explore the creativity of the evangelists in their respective interpretations of the traditions about Jesus' words and deeds.[3] Applied to the beatitudes, this approach aims to hear these sayings as Matthew and Luke interpret them.

Many non-professional students of the Bible (and even some professionals) find this approach threatening. For to the extent

---

[1]The starting point for any in-depth study of the beatitudes remains the magisterial three-volume work of J. Dupont, *Les Béatitudes*; I. Le problème litteraire—les deux versions du Sermon sur la montagne et des Béatitudes (2nd ed; Louvaine: E. Nauwelaerts, 1958); II. La Bonne Nouvelle (Paris: J. Gabalda, 1969); III. Les Evangelistes (Paris: J. Gabalda, 1973). The fruit of this work found non-technical expression in two summary articles of Dupont: "L'interpretation des Béatitudes," *Foi et Vie* 65 (1966) 17-39, and "Introduction aux Béatitudes," *NRT* 98 (1976) 97-108. Some recent helpful studies in English are R. Guelich, "The Matthean Beatitudes: 'Entrance-Requirements' or Eschatological Blessings?" *JBL* 95 (1976) 415-434 and Guelich's fully developed commentary, *The Sermon On the Mount* (Waco, TX: Word Books, 1982), esp. 62-118; N. McEleney, "The Beatitudes of the Sermon on the Mount/Plain," *CBQ* 43 (1981) 1-13; J. Lambrecht, *The Sermon on the Mount: Proclamation and Exhortation* (Wilmington, DE: Michael Glazier, 1985), esp. 45-79.

[2]See, for example, H. Cazelles, "*'Ashre*," *TDOT* 1 (1974) 445-448; F. Hauck and Bertram, "*Makarios, makarizo, makarismos*," *TDNT* 4 (1967) 362-370; W.Janzen, "*'ashre* in the Old Testament," *HTR* 58 (1965) 215-226.

[3]The approaches of Dupont, Guelich, and Lambrecht are exemplary in their treatments of the evangelists' editing of the beatitudes. This brief study presumes and builds upon their work and intends to contribute to an even fuller hearing of the beatitudes in their full gospel contexts.

we focus on the sayings of Jesus *as told by* Matthew and *as told by* Luke, to that extent we may seem to be distancing ourselves from the words of Jesus. The evangelist appears to intervene. The more redaction critics find signs of the mind of Matthew or the hand of Luke, the more some Christian readers feel themselves removed from the word of the Lord.

That may be an inevitable *initial* response to redaction or composition criticism. It has been my own experience, however, that the more seriously I take the evangelists as authors creatively "midwifing" the tradition for their believing readers, the more confidence I have been led to place in their fidelity to the meaning of Jesus as risen Lord of the church. Luke and Matthew passed on the received traditions about the words and deeds of Jesus in the ways they thought would best help their contemporaries live the faith. The church recognized this with magisterial formality when, after three centuries of experience, we canonized our four versions of the story of Jesus and definitively recognized their place at the center of our life and worship.

Understood properly, it is not an act of fundamentalist regression to say that the best commentary on the beatitudes of Jesus is the Old Testament (the primary source of their imagery) and the full gospel texts in which those beatitudes are found. For if Jesus spoke with unaccustomed authority and striking boldness, he did so in the traditional language of his Jewish heritage. And if the evangelists reverently passed on the traditions of Jesus of Nazareth in their proclamations of him as risen Lord, they were also careful to fashion a literary framework to help us interpret that tradition. To ignore that framework is to risk misunderstanding.

Accordingly, the aim of this small book is to help us hear the familiar beatitudes afresh by attending to their Old Testament background and under the new light shed by the study of their immediate literary context. The focus throughout will be to hear the beatitudes of Jesus as understood by their most authoritative interpreters, Matthew and Luke.

As to content, the book is arranged in three parts. (1) Part one explores some questions preliminary to our study of the beatitudes in their gospel settings. What is a beatitude? How might Jesus' words have been heard before Easter? What are we to make of the variations between Matthew's and Luke's versions? (2) Since many commentators judge that Luke's presentation of the beatitudes is closer to the pre-Gospel tradition, part two begins our study of individual beatitudes with Luke's four beatitudes and their corresponding "woes." Our main effort will be to hear them "as told by Luke" within his version of the story of Jesus. (3) Part three will do the same for the beatitudes according to Matthew. In an afterword, I will present some final reflections flowing from this study.

Part One

Some Preliminary Questions

I. What's a Macarism?

When Jesus used the language pattern, "Blessed [are] those who ...," he was using a formula that would have had a familiar ring in the ears of his synagogue-going listeners. This holds true for the readers and audiences of Matthew and Luke, people who would have been familiar with the Hebrew Scriptures, whether in the original language (Hebrew), or in Aramaic (the vernacular of Palestine in Jesus' day), or in the Greek version. For this form of expression occurs in several books of the Old Testament, most frequently in the wisdom books (especially Proverbs and Sirach) and in the Psalms (some twenty-six times).[1]

By the time of Jesus, what we call a beatitude (from the Latin *beatus*, "fortunate") was a recognizable form in the minds of the educated. The Greeks, as usual, had a word for it, *makarismos*, which is the noun form of the adjective whose plural form begins each of the classical gospel beatitudes: *makarioi* ("fortunate," "happy," "blessed")[2] are the poor, etc.

---

[1] It has become customary, out of sensitivity to our Jewish brothers and sisters, to refer to the Old Testament as the Hebrew Bible. Since, however, the evangelists more often use the Greek version of the Hebrew Bible, and the name "Hebrew Bible" seems to refer to the text in the original Hebrew language, I shall normally use the term Old Testament (abbrev. OT) in this book.

Indeed, the word macarism has even found its way into modern languages as a technical term for beatitude.

It will help our discussion of the gospel beatitudes if we take a moment to look at the shape of the OT macarism tradition which Jesus and the NT writers inherited. First, a general description of the form, then some examples, and then some observations about the function of that literary type.

The form.

The typical OT beatitude has several constants:

(a) the adjective *'ashre* in Hebrew, or *makarios/makarioi* in Greek, meaning, in both cases, "blessed" or "fortunate";

(b) a subject (normally indicated in the third person, "the one who . . .") whose behavior or whose happy state is described in a relative or participial clause; and finally, sometimes a third element closely associated with the first two:

(c) a description that elaborates either the blessed state or the piety that led to this happy condition.

Regarding element(a), the Hebrew word *'ashre* is, in the OT, always applied to a human being by a human being, never by God or to God.[3] The adjective is better translated "blessed" rather than simply "happy" or "fortunate" because, as we will see from our examples, what is described is never simply the subjective emotional state of the individual but rather a situation deriving from that person's relationship with God. A beatitude is an acknowledgement of that relationship. When the Hebrew Bible was done into Greek a couple of centuries B.C., the word chosen to translate *'ashre*, i.e. *makarios*, was most apt. For already in Hellenistic Greek, the word had divine associations. Homer called the Greek gods *makarioi*; then, by extension, human beings were sometimes called *makarioi* when they were thought of as participating in

---

[2] *"Blessed, fortunate, happy,* usu. in the sense *privileged recipient of divine favor"* is the initial entry under *makarios* in W. Bauer, W. Arndt, F. Gingrich, and F. Danker, *A Greek-English Lexicon of the New Testament and Other Early Christian Literature* (Chicago: University of Chicago, 1979), 486. [Hereafter this lexicon will be referred to as BAGD.]

[3] See W. Janzen, "*'Ashre* in the Old Testament," 224.

the happiness of the gods. Thus, as a consequence of the meanings associated with both the Hebrew *'ashre* and the Greek *makarios*, calling someone *'ashre* or *makarios* is always a religious statement. It is an assertion about that person's happy state with respect to God.[4]

As for the second element (b), the application of the quality "blessed" to the subject occurs without the verb "to be." In Hebrew that omission is due simply to the fact that the verb for "being" or "becoming" is not normally used as a linking verb. Interestingly, that Hebrew pattern carries over into the Greek versions of the OT and NT macarisms, which usually say "*makarioi hoi* such and such" ("blessed: the such and such") and not "*makarioi estin hoi* such and such" ("blessed *are* the such and such").

Some examples.

Paul, in Rom 4, presents us with an excellent example of an Old Testament beatitude, and he even *calls* it a macarism. In his discussion of faith versus works of the Law, he quotes Ps 32. He says:

> So also David pronounces a blessing upon [*legei ton makarismon*, literally, "says a macarism to"] the one to whom God reckons righteousness apart from works:
> "Blessed [*makarioi*] [are] those whose iniquities are
>   forgiven, and whose sins are covered;
>   blessed [is] the one [*makarios anēr*] against whom the
>   Lord will not reckon his sin."
> Is this blessing [*makarismos*] pronounced only upon the circumcised, or also upon the uncircumcised?

Each of these two beatitudes in Paul's quotation from Ps 32:1-2 provides a showcase example of the first two components in the generalized formula for OT beatitudes outlined above: (a) it begins with the predicative *makarios* (*'ashre* in the original Hebrew of the quoted psalm); (b) it asserts that blessedness, without the help of the "is" verb, of a person

---

[4]See F. Hauck and Bertram, "*Makarios, makarizō, makarismos,*" 362.

whose happiness is described in a clause. Note that the blessedness is, in both cases, a matter of being on the receiving end of a divine action.

The very first psalm in the psalter provides another important example of the OT beatitude format:

> Blessed is the man who walks not
>   in the counsel of the wicked,
> nor stands in the way of sinners,
>   nor sits in the seat of scoffers;
> but his delight is in the law of the Lord,
>   and on his law he meditates day and night.
> He is like a tree planted by streams of water,
> that yields its fruit in its season,
>   and its leaf does not wither.

Here the (b)-component describes the behavior of the person, and the (c)-element ("He is like a tree . . .") expands on the condition of blessedness resulting from the pious behavior. The second stanza, vv 4-6, describes the opposite lot of the wicked, expanded with an organic image of fruitless impermanence.

Similar examples from the Psalms abound. The whole of Ps 112 develops the opening macarism ("Blessed is the one who fears the Lord, who greatly delights in his commandments!") by spelling out the consequences of that piety: mighty descendants, wealth, good reputation, victory over foes. See also the blessings elaborated in Pss 127:5 (sons), 128:1-6 (children), 144:12-15 (children, flock, and crops for those whose god is the Lord).

Sirach 25:7-11 is a striking development of the beatitude tradition in that it provides a list of earthly goods that render a person fit to be called *makarios* (friends, downfall of enemies, a sensible and compatible spouse, an attentive friend, wisdom), and then the sage climaxes the list by naming the gift that is considered the source of those blessings, fear of the Lord: "And fear of the Lord surpasses everything; to whom shall be likened the one who holds it fast?" The elements of gift and response in this description of beatitude relationship with God are elements that will become important in Jesus' use of the beatitude tradition.

Up to now we have been considering the *format* of OT beatitudes. With respect to the *content*, scholars commonly distinguish between wisdom beatitudes and apocalyptic beatitudes.[5] *Wisdom* beatitudes focus on attitudes and behavior valuable for one's personal well-being in the here and now. *Apocalyptic* beatitudes, on the other hand, focus on attitudes and behaviors which find their reward in God's future intervention into history. Note that the examples of OT beatitudes treated above are examples of wisdom beatitudes. Apparently the earliest biblical example of the apocalyptic macarism is Dan 12:12-13: "Blessed is he who waits and comes to the thousand three hundred and thirty-five days." The next verse elaborates on the futurity: "But go your way till the end; and you shall rest, and shall stand in your allotted place at the end of days." Most of the forty-four New Testament macarisms are apocalyptic beatitudes. Witness Jas 1:12: "Happy the man who holds out to the end through trial! Once he has been proved, he will receive the crown of life the Lord has promised to those who love him."

Notice that wisdom beatitudes and apocalyptic beatitudes are very much alike. Both acknowledge as blessed the person who seeks to do God's will (fears God, loves God). The wisdom beatitude highlights the goods of "this age," whereas the apocalyptic macarism, the goods of the "age to come," but in both cases, what is affirmed is a *blessed relationship with God in the present*, quite apart from the questions of when the *fullness* of the relationship is to be experienced.

II. What Does a Macarism Do?

So much for the form and content. Let us now look at the function. What is the point of a macarism? What is the rhetorical purpose of the one who speaks or writes a beatitude?

---

[5]See for example Klaus Koch, *The Growth of the Biblical Tradition* (London: Adam & Chas. Black, 1969) 17-18.

From the examples we have seen, I submit that we can make this generalization: a beatitude is a kind of congratulation, spoken by one human being to another (not God to human or human to God),[6] the purpose being to affirm, encourage and hold up as example those qualities for which the person is congratulated. Psalm 1, for example, is a prologue to the whole psalter. Obviously its purpose in predicating *'ashre* (or *makarios*) the person who "delights in the way of the Lord" and comparing him or her to a permanently fruitful tree (and, on the other hand, comparing the wicked person to chaff which the wind drives away) is not simply to observe an interesting fact. Such a communiqué is clearly meant to persuade the reader (or listener or worshipper or psalm-singer) to delight in the Law of the Lord and to meditate on this law day and night. Praise has the social function of promoting those values and behaviors which the community holds dear (or at least what the *speaker* holds dear; in the case of the biblical macarisms, because they are in the canon of Scripture, we know that they affirm the values held by the canonizing community).

The point of biblical macarisms may become clearer when we realize that most advertisements in today's media are, at bottom, secular beatitudes. The TV iconography of the retired home-run hitter enjoying a cool, sparkling mug of a certain beer is, at heart, a macarism. The message of the commercial might be paraphrased: "Happy those who drink 'Old ——'! They not only quench their thirst. They also place themselves in the company of the likes of this all-time great." With respect to content, such an ad purports to be of the wisdom variety. Like most biblical beatitudes, the point of a secular macarism is to get you to do something. As we shall see, there is more to the beatitudes of Jesus than that, but it is important to recognize the tradition with which he and the evangelists work.

---

[6]W. Janzen, "*'Ashre* in the Old Testament," 224. This in fact is what distinguishes an *'ashre* saying (or beatitude) from a *baruch* saying (or blessing), which is normally by or about God.

III. A First Reading: Questioning the Texts

Since we shall be spending a substantial amount of time considering a set of brief texts, we will do well to take a moment simply reading those texts afresh, observing what meets the eye and ear and acknowledging whatever questions surface spontaneously. What follows is the English translation called the Revised Standard Version, which I use because it is a very close rendering of the original Greek. Where the RSV translation uses words for which there is no literal counterpart in the Greek original (e.g., the verb "are" after "blessed") I have dropped them. To facilitate comparison, the versions of Matthew and Luke are printed in parallel columns. "People" or "they" replace the RSV's "men" where the Greek is more inclusive.

Mt 5:3-12	Lk 6:20b-26
3 Blessed: the poor in spirit, for theirs is the kingdom of heaven.	20b Blessed: the poor for yours is the kingdom of God.
4 Blessed: those who mourn, for they shall be comforted.	
5 Blessed: the meek, for they shall inherit the earth.	
6 Blessed: those who hunger and thirst for righteousness, for they shall be satisfied.	21 Blessed: those who hunger now, for you shall be satisfied. Blessed: those who weep now, for you shall laugh.
7 Blessed: the merciful, for they shall obtain mercy.	
8 Blessed: the pure in heart, for they shall see God.	
9 Blessed: the peacemakers, for they shall be called sons of God.	

10 Blessed: those who are
persecuted for
righteousness' sake,
for theirs is the kingdom
of heaven.

11 Blessed are you when they
revile you and persecute
you and utter all kinds
of evil against you falsely
on my account.

22 Blessed are you when
people hate you, and
when they exclude you
and revile you,
and cast out your name as
evil, on account of the
Son of man!

12 Rejoice and be glad, for
your reward is great in
heaven, for so they per-
secuted the prophets who
were before you.

23 Rejoice on that day, and
leap for joy, for behold,
your reward is great in
heaven; for so their
fathers did to the
prophets.

24 But woe to you that are
rich, for you have
received your consolation.
25 Woe to you that are full
now, for you shall hunger.
Woe to those that laugh
now for you shall mourn
and weep.
26 Woe when all speak well
of you, for so their fathers
did to the false prophets.

First, let us begin to think about these texts by observing
the obvious, the things virtually every commentator says when
asked to account for the similarities and differences of these

two versions of the beatitudes of Jesus.[7] Matthew gives us nine beatitudes, eight of them cast in the form of the third person plural and a ninth, apparently expanding on the eighth, addressed in the second person ("you," in the plural, we discover when we look at the Greek). Luke, on the other hand, gives us four beatitudes, roughly paralleling Matthew's first, second, fourth and ninth in content; in addition, Luke gives us four "woes" that articulate the "other side" of his four beatitudes.

Several other details of form and content emerge in this initial comparison. Whereas the first eight of Matthew's beatitudes are spoken in the third person, in Luke's beatitudes, only the kernels ("Blessed the poor," "Blessed the thirsting," "Blessed the weeping now") of the first three have the third person form.[8] But all the Lucan motive clauses ("for yours is the kingdom of God," etc.), the whole of the fourth beatitude, and three of the woes are spoken in the *second* person plural. Moreover, in Luke's second and third beatitudes and second and third woes, there is an expressed contrast between the *now* of the hungry and the weepers and their *future* bliss, and between the *now* of the full and laughing and their *future* hunger, mourning, and weeping

Whereas the Lucan Jesus congratulates the poor and the hungry, the Matthean Jesus congratulates the poor *in spirit* and those who hunger *and thirst for righteousness*.

As Luke's version has a balanced pattern (four macarisms matched by four woes), Matthew has his internal patterns: the explanatory clauses of the first and eighth are identical ("for theirs is the kingdom of heaven") and thus serve to frame the unit of eight; the eighth also patterns with the fourth by echoing the theme of righteousness.

In each list, the *last* beatitude—Matthew's ninth (Mt 5:11-

---

[7]See, for example, the works already cited by J. Dupont, R. A. Guelich, N. McEleney, or, recently, J. A. Fitzmyer, *The Gospel According to Luke (I-IX)* (AB 28; Garden City, NY: Doubleday, 1981) 624-646; and G. Beasley-Murray, *Jesus and the Kingdom of God* (Grand Rapids: Eerdmans, 1986) 156-169.

[8]The fact that the kernels of the first three Lucan beatitudes occur, like Matthew's, in the *third* person form is obscured by virtually all translations, which, quite reasonably, harmonize the expression of the kernels with the second person form of the motive clauses.

12) and Luke's fourth (Lk 6:22-23)—is similar: in both lists it occurs in the third person plural and consists of two verses, the first being a straightforward macarism and the second giving two motive clauses after a brief exhortation ("rejoice [Mt: and be glad] [Lk: on that day] for your reward is great in heaven, for so they did to the prophets . . .").

Certain features of the larger context are also worth observing at the outset. In both gospels, the beatitudes form the preface of a major speech of similar content, spoken early in his public ministry (in Matthew it is Jesus' first major speech; in Luke it is his second). In both cases the setting of the words is associated with a mountain (*on* the mount in Matthew; on a level place at the *foot* of a mountain in Luke). In both gospels the beatitudes are preceded by references to Jesus' healing ministry and a gathering of people from a wide geographical area.

IV. A Version Behind the Versions: The "Q" Beatitudes

These considerations place us unavoidably in the presence of what is classically known as "the synoptic problem." At the same time, the beatitudes also offer the basis of the classical solution to the synoptic problem, the two-source theory. While this brief volume is not the place to review this scholarly discussion in its full complexity, some of the questions inevitably raised by a close study of the beatitudes demand attention.

The basic question underlying the complex of issues conventionally labeled the synoptic problem is this: given the fact that the Gospels called Matthew, Mark, and Luke present the story of Jesus in essentially the same outline, and given that all three have much material in common, along with striking differences, can we posit a theory of relationships among these texts which accounts for both their similarities and differences? A primary insight leading to the most widely accepted solution to that question ("the two-source theory") was the recognition that, while Matthew and Luke share a narrative line quite similar to Mark, they also have in common a substantial body of material (mainly sayings of Jesus) which does *not* appear in Mark. Moreover, this material common to Matthew and Luke appears in their respective Gospels in roughly the same sequence but often in different settings and arrangements. These observations led to the theory that Matthew and Luke had access to a source not used by Mark. Since the common material has virtually identical vocabulary and a similar sequence, it was judged that the source was a written document featuring sayings of Jesus. Since German scholars first developed the theory, this hypothetical sayings document was dubbed "Q" (standing for *Quelle*, the German word for "source"). Given that a literary relationship between Mark and Matthew and Luke seemed obvious, and since it seemed unlikely that anyone would abbreviate Matthew or Luke by cutting out major parables and key sayings of Jesus, it seemed best to assume that Mark wrote first, without access to the sayings tradition represented by "Q". It was easy, then, to imagine that Matthew and Luke, working independently of one another, each used the same two sources for the bulk of their respective Gospels: they each used some version of Mark for the essential narrative and into their retelling of the story of Jesus according to Mark, they introduced the sayings of Jesus they knew from "Q". Matthew did this mainly by building the five major speeches of his Gospel, and Luke presented Jesus speaking many of those sayings during the long journey to Jerusalem that comprises the extensive central section of his Gospel (Lk 9:51-19:27).

Once this theory was established as a way of accounting for the relationships among the first three Gospels, it became all the more important to account for the *differences* in Matthew's and Luke's transmission of their shared tradition. That led to the fruitful enterprise of *redaction criticism*, the study of the Gospels which examines evidence of the special "editorial interests" evidenced by the evangelists' reworking of their received traditions. It soon became apparent that the variations among the evangelists were not the random variations one might expect from a variety of human witnesses; those variations proved rather to be stunningly coherent expressions of thematic concerns of their authors. In short, the variations proved to be not random and trivial but deliberate and deeply meaningful.

Against the background of the two-source hypothesis, it is

obvious that the beatitudes are a prime example of the need for such a theory and an illustration of its usefulness. For in Mt 5:3-12 and Lk 6:20b-23 we have material which is lacking in Mark but which Matthew and Luke share. Moreover, the variations (additions, omissions, and alterations) have such a patterned character that they suggest not the accidental variations of oral transmission but deliberate remodeling by the evangelists themselves. Within the hypothesis of a "Q" document, then, the four beatitudes which Matthew and Luke have in common (blessed are the poor, blessed are the hungering, blessed are the weeping/mourning, blessed are you when they revile you) are "Q" material.

The next question which arises naturally is this: can we make a good guess at the wording of those four macarisms as Matthew and Luke would have found them in "Q"? Using common sense, the two-source theory, and a general familiarity with the gospels of Matthew and Luke, the intelligent reader can duplicate most of the conjectures of contemporary scholarly opinion on this subject.

Most guesses about the "Q" version of the four common beatitudes go like this:

> Blessed [are] the poor,
> for theirs is the kingdom of God.

Matthew's *in spirit*, as we shall argue later, is Matthean interpretation. Luke's "kingdom *of God*" is more likely to be the original phrasing than Matthew's "kingdom *of heaven*," for "kingdom of heaven" is a special preference of Matthew's throughout his gospel. As regards the originality of Matthew's "for theirs" over Luke's "for yours," Matthew's third-person expression of the motive clause fits the literary form of the beatitude more naturally, whereas Luke's shift from the second person of the kernel to the second person of the motive clause introduces a strain, the very thing which prompts virtually all translators to smooth things over by introducing "are you" into the kernel. Moreover, Luke shows a preference for the second-person throughout his Gospel.

> Blessed [are] the hungering,
> for they shall be satisfied.

Matthew's "and thirst for righteousness" is best understood as his addition, for *righteousness* is a thematic word in Matthew; it is used seven times in his gospel (five of these in the Sermon on the Mount, and twice in his version of the beatitudes). The Lucan order of the first three beatitudes (poor/hungry/weeping) is more likely to be original than the Matthean (poor/mourning/hungry) because poor-and-hungry are a common pair in the language of the Hebrew tradition.

> Blessed [are] those who mourn,
> for they shall be comforted.

While Luke's weeping and laughing are more concrete than Matthew's mourning and being consoled (and one might think a change from weeping to mourning consistént with the change from *poor* to *poor in spirit*), other details suggest the originality of Matthew's mourning: in the consequence of Luke's first woe, he speaks of *consolation* [*paraklēsis*] and in the consequence of his third woe he includes mourning along with weeping, which suggests that he here reflects the "Q" version of the beatitude about those who mourn, which Matthew presents as the second one in his list.

> Blessed are you when they hate you and revile you and utter evil of you on account of the Son of Man. Rejoice and be glad, for your reward is great in heaven, for so they did to the prophets.[9]

This final beatitude differs from the other three in two striking ways: first, in both gospels, it is expressed in the second-person ("blessed are *you*"); second, its content deals explicitly with the theme of being a disciple of Jesus. Indeed, it is only the juxtaposition of the last beatitude with the other three which gives the others a Christian meaning.

[9]This reconstruction of the of last Q-beatitude is that of J. Lambrecht, *The Sermon on the Mount*, 50-51. It was arrived at by removing language which is judged, by way of comparison with the respective author's typical vocabulary, to come from the hand of the evangelist. Thus, "in that day," "leap for joy," and "behold" are taken to be Lucan additions, and the verb for "persecute" is, because of Matthew's interest in that motif, ascribed to that evangelist. Luke's apparent allusion to formal exclusion of Jewish-Christians from the synagogue (*aphorisōsin*) reflects a later time than the more informal hostility reflected in the Gospel of Matthew.

Even if we are convinced that we have made a good guess at the expression that the four common beatitudes might have had in their "Q" document form, there remains the question, Do we have here the *ipsissima verba* (the actual words) of Jesus? About the first three, few commentators have doubted that they are sayings of Jesus. Some scholars have attributed the last beatitude to Stage Two of the transmission of the gospel tradition (the period of the post-Easter preaching and teaching of the church). The reason: rejection of Jesus' followers does not become an urgent topic until after Easter. On the other hand, it is not out of the question that Jesus, reading the signs of the times, might have spoken such words as he approached the final crisis in Jerusalem.

Now that we have guessed our way back to the version of the beatitudes as they might have been spoken by Jesus, we are teased by the inevitable question, How might Jesus himself have expected these words to have been understood by his early first-century Palestinian listeners in those pre-Christian days of his earthly ministry?

V. The Beatitudes' Meaning in Jesus' Ministry

Although the purpose of our study is to understand Matthew's and Luke's interpretations of the beatitudes, it makes sense at least to try to hear the beatitudes as they might have been heard by Jesus' contemporaries during his earthly ministry. We begin with the first three and save the last for later.

> Blessed are the poor,
>   for theirs is the kingdom of God.
> Blessed are the mourning,
>   for they shall be consoled.
> Blessed are the hungering,
>   for they shall be satisfied.

When the first three "Q" beatitudes are presented in isolation, their parallelism stands out clearly. The subjects, those who are congratulated—the poor, the mourning, and the hungering—are not three distinct groups but really three descriptions of the same people. The poor (the *anawim* in Hebrew, *hoi ptōchoi* in Greek: those so wretched they are forced to beg) are inevitably mourning and hungry.

As regards the second member of each of the verses, the promise, the reason for congratulation is expressed in three parallel phrases whose content is also synonymous. Each promise refers to an act of God. In the second and the third promise, the comforter and the satisfier is God, for putting a verb in the passive voice is a typical Semitic way of naming an action of God ("Knock and it will be opened to you"—Mt 7:7).

As for the promise of the first macarism, "for theirs is the kingdom of God,"—just how that speaks of an action of God demands some explanation. Here I shall try to summarize briefly the results of a rich contemporary discussion in NT scholarship.[10]

The Kingdom (or Reign) of God was the centerpiece of Jesus' preaching and story telling. The phrase is a metaphor. To speak of God's kingdom or reign is to take the image of king from human social life and apply it to God. God can be thought of as being king-like in that God is the ultimate authority, the one exercising judgment, responsible for the public order, the common good, the defense of the people, the care of the poor.

Jesus used that image in a peculiar way. Each of the synoptic Gospels summarizes his preaching with the sentence, "The Kingdom of God is *at hand.*" At the same time, he taught his disciples to pray for the *coming* of the Kingdom in the prayer to God as Father. At first this seems an odd use of the image of God as king. If you imagine God as a king, then of course God's reigning is something of the past and the present as well as future. If it is the *nature* of a king to reign, why, then, speak of the Kingdom of God as being *at hand* or *coming*? This way of speaking is a special use of the image of God's royal power; it is a theme from apocalyptic literature.

---

[10]For representative reviews of the topic, see N. Perrin, *Jesus and the Language of the Kingdom* (Philadelphia: Fortress, 1976) and I. H. Marshall, "The Hope of a New Age: The Kingdom of God in the New Testament," *Themelios* 11 (1985) 5-15.

Apocalyptic writers thought this way: in this "present age," *other* kings than God and other kingdoms—the Persian, the Greek, the Roman—were having their day and holding their sway, while God was apparently hiding the full force of his reign; but in "the age to come," God the King would clearly show his reign by a decisive intervention in human history with signs, wonders, the advent of the Messiah, an outpouring of the Spirit, reward for the righteous and judgment for the wicked.

Jesus' listeners would have recognized that he was using "Kingdom of God" in the apocalyptic mode and that he was announcing "the age to come." And yet, they would have sensed that Jesus was not simply repeating the apocalyptic view; he was using Kingdom-of-God talk as a rich, flexible *symbol* to proclaim that the expected coming Reign of God was already showing itself in his person and ministry.

This link (between the reign of God and the person and ministry of Jesus) is asserted in two other "Q" sayings of Jesus. Defending himself against the charge of working demonic deliverance by satanic power, he says, "But if it is by the Spirit of God [Luke: the finger of God] that I cast out demons, then the reign of God has overtaken you" (Mt 12:28; par. Lk 11:20). Note that the context speaks of the *end* of another reign, the reign of Satan.

On another occasion, in response to the embassy sent by the imprisoned John the Baptist, Jesus said, "Go back and tell John what you hear and see; the blind receive their sight and the lame walk, lepers are cleansed and the deaf hear, and the dead are raised up, and the poor have the good news preached to them. And blessed is he who takes no offense at me" (Mt 11:4-6; par. Lk 7:22-23). Several things should be observed here. (1) Jesus' response is not a direct quotation but a collage of allusions to several end-time passages in Isaiah: 35:5-6 (blind see, deaf hear), 29:18-19 (deaf hear, blind see, poor [*anawim=ptōchoi* LXX] rejoice), and climaxing with an explicit echo of 61:1—("the Lord has anointed me to bring good tidings to the afflicted" [*anawim*; LXX: *ptōchoi*, "poor," "lowly"]). (2) Jesus' answer ends in a beatitude focusing on response to himself.

In these verses, then, Jesus interprets his healing ministry with the language in which Isaiah speaks of end-time redemption, which Jesus' audience would have associated with the expected intervention of the Reign of God. Moreover, he explicitly identifies himself with the messenger of Is 61. To appreciate what this means, it will be helpful to hear a full quotation of the Isaian passage (I give the RSV translation of the Hebrew [and, in brackets, where the variation is significant, a literal rendering of the Greek version, whose sign, by the way, is LXX, standing for its name, The Septuagint]):

> The Spirit of the Lord God is upon me,
>> because the Lord has anointed me
>> to bring good tidings to the afflicted [Hebrew: *anawim;*
>>> LXX: *ptōchoi,* poor]
>> he has sent me to bind up the brokenhearted,
>> to proclaim liberty to the captives,
>>> and the opening of the prison to those who are bound;
>> [LXX: and recovery of sight to the blind]
>> to proclaim the year of the Lord's favor,
>>> and the day of vengeance of our God;
>>> to comfort all who mourn;
>> to grant to those who mourn in Zion—
>>> to give them a garland instead of ashes,
>> the oil of gladness instead of mourning,
>>> the mantle of praise instead of a faint spirit;
>> that they may be called oaks of righteousness,
>> the planting of the Lord, that he may be glorified.

❧ ✳ ❦

> Instead of your shame you shall have a double portion,
> [LXX: Thus they shall inherit the land a second time,
> *ek deuteras klēronomēsousi tēn gēn*]
>> instead of dishonor you shall rejoice in your lot;
> therefore in your land you shall possess a double portion;
>> yours shall be everlasting joy. (Is 61:1-4,7)

There is good reason to believe that when we read this Isaian text, we have arrived at the "home" of the beatitudes, both in ministry of Jesus and in the minds of the evangelists.

To return to our effort to hear the beatitudes in their setting in Jesus' ministry, we realize now that they were not presented in a vacuum but in the environment of Jesus' healing and preaching ministry interpreted by language of Isaiah understood apocalyptically.[11] The first three "Q" macarisms sound very Isaian indeed. As in Is 61, the poor and the mourning are the recipients of glad tidings. And we do not have to look far in the same prophetic scroll for references to the hungry getting filled in the endtime redemption (see Is 61:6; cf. 25:6; 55:1-3; 65:13-14).[12]

Abstracted from the context of his ministry and of the OT allusions, the statement "The Kingdom of God is theirs" could be taken simply as a reference to the future (similar to "your reward is great in heaven"), in parallel with the promises of the two other "Q" beatitudes ("they shall be satisfied" . . . "they shall be consoled"). But the explicit linking of the Kingdom of God with the healing ministry in the "Q" sayings in Mt 11:4-6 and 12:28 suggests that the present tense of the first beatitude is meant to be taken seriously. In Jesus' person and work the future Reign of God has been inaugurated and rendered accessible.

To his Palestinian peers, Jesus must have sounded as if he were saying, in effect: Happy the poor, the hungry, the mourning; the more you know your need for God, the more you shall be open to God's end-time Reign, which is beginning to happen already—in my healing, my teaching, and in my gathering of the outcast in table fellowship.

On the face of it, Jesus was issuing traditional apocalyptic

---

[11]For evidence of first-century Jewish interpretation of Is 61 as an end-time passage (i.e. in the Qumran document, 11Q Melchizedek), see Robert B. Sloan, *The Favorable Year of the Lord: A Study of Jubilary Theology in the Gospel of Luke* (Austin, TX: Schola, 1977) esp. pp. 43-44.

[12]Our modern distinction between pre-exilic First Isaiah (chaps. 1-39), exilic Second Isaiah (chaps. 40-55), and post-exilic Third Isaiah (56-66) need not prevent us from assuming that the first-century readers of the scroll of Isaiah would have thought of it as a unified work. Indeed, contemporary literary study of Isaiah is demonstrating that the school of Isaiah itself, in the course of its two-century work of incremental interpretation, used imagery of chapters 1-39 in chapters 40-55, and imagery from chapters 1-55 in chapters 56-66. For recent discussions of this approach to the literary integrity of Isaiah, see Richard Clifford, *Fair Spoken and Persuading: An Interpretation of Second Isaiah* (New York: Paulist, 1984) and Elizabeth Achtemeier, *The Community and Message of Isaiah 56-66* (Minneapolis: Augsburg, 1982).

beatitudes. But in the context of his kingdom preaching and healing ministry, these beatitudes outstrip the traditional function of exhortation. The center of gravity has shifted. The point is now proclamation. The expected Reign of God is now accessible. The exhortation to repent simply follows from that good news.

As for the last beatitude, although many commentators attribute this tradition to Stage Two of the transmission of the gospel tradition (that is, the period of the post-Easter apostolic preaching), it is not impossible that Jesus spoke something like this toward the end of his public ministry, when he was preparing his close disciples for sharing in the dire consequences of his ministry.[13] Even before Easter, Jesus' Palestinian auditors would have perceived a continuity with the other beatitudes. Those who identify with the end-time Prophet will share in the double lot proper to prophets generally, and to the Isaian Servant of Yahweh especially: (1) human rejection and (2) divine vindication.[14]

When Luke and Matthew transmit the "Q" beatitudes, each in his own way shows that he is aware of the Isaian background. Each fills in the blanks for the reader. Matthew does it by retrieving (or constructing) five other beatitudes and aligning them with the primary base, Is 61; Luke does it by introducing an extensive quotation of Is 61 (with 58:6) into his version of Jesus' inaugural sermon at Nazareth (Lk 4:18-19). Both writers, we shall see, are creatively faithful to what appears to have been the original thrust of those macarisms in Jesus' preaching, as each interprets them in ways that are directed toward the faith life of their respective communities. To those interpretations we now turn.

[13]See I. H. Marshall, *The Gospel of Luke* (Grand Rapids: Eerdmans, 1978) 252.

[14]See E. Achtemeier (*Community and Message of Isaiah 56-66*, 88-94) on the continuity between the prophet of Trito-Isaiah and the Servant of Second Isaiah.

Part Two

The Beatitudes (and Woes)
According to Luke

We shall begin with Luke, for two reasons: first, Luke's beatitudes are closest to the Q version; second, the context provided by the Third Gospel makes the most explicit reference to the most obvious OT background of the beatitudes, Is 61 (at 4:18 and, by way of allusion, 7:22).

When we meet the beatitudes in the Third Gospel, we are already more than five chapters into the story. The author has carefully prepared the reader by introducing the speaker of the beatitudes and the audience to whom they are addressed. He has, moreover, given us an interpretation of the moment in sacred history in which these words are spoken. Then, once the beatitudes and woes are uttered, they, in turn, provide part of the background against which the rest of the story of Jesus and the church are to be heard. Accordingly, our method for exploring Luke's interpretation of the beatitudes will be to take pains to hear carefully those words as they occur in, and are informed by, the story of Jesus and the church as Luke tells it. We shall ask, Who is talking? To whom is he speaking? What time (of history) is it? What is he saying? And how does the rest of the story help us understand what he is saying?

I. Who is Talking?

It is widely recognized that the infancy narrative of Lk 1-2 comprises an overture introducing not only the Third Gospel but the Acts of the Apostles as well. The author is beginning a two-volume whole. Indeed, some of the themes asserted about Jesus in these early chapters ("the Lord will give him the throne of David his father," 1:32; "... a light for revelation to the Gentiles ...," 2:32) find their fulfillment only in Acts (see Acts 2:29-31 and 26:22-23). To hear Luke's beatitudes within the sweep of that story, we must attend to his narrative carefully. How does Luke present Jesus in the five and two-fifths chapters preceding the beatitudes and woes of the Sermon on the Plain? We shall review those initial chapters with special attention to the titles which Luke uses to interpret the person of Jesus.

A) SON OF GOD

Jesus is announced by Gabriel as one to be called "Son of the Most High" (v 32) and this filiation is clarified; it is because he will be conceived by the Holy Spirit, the Power of the Most High, that he will be called Son of God.[1] Already, the title Son of God is clearly more than messianic. Divine sonship is reaffirmed when, after the baptism of Jesus and "all the people," Jesus is at prayer and the Holy Spirit descended upon him (*in bodily form* Luke adds, since he had already mentioned the participation of the Holy Spirit in Jesus' conception) and the voice from heaven says, "Thou art my beloved Son; with thee I am well pleased." The first half of the statement, the divine declaration of sonship, is very likely an allusion to Ps 2:7, one of the royal psalms; this would specify Jesus' sonship as somehow

---

[1]That Son of God also functions as a messianic title for Luke is apparent for the equation with the title Christ at Lk 4:41 (where demons call him Son of God and he rebukes them, "because they knew that he was the Christ") and Acts 9:20,22 (where Paul's preaching is epitomized as saying "He is the Son of God" and two verses later as "proving that Jesus was the Christ").

kingly. The second half of the declaration ("with thee I am
well pleased") seems to allude to the first servant song in
Isaiah (42:1), thereby interpreting Jesus with Isaiah's figure
of a prophetic leader who both represents Israel and
ministers to Israel as a suffering and obedient servant of
God.

This heavenly declaration at the Jordan receives further
interpretation from what follows in Luke's narrative. The
genealogy (3:23-38) works backward from Joseph, through
David, and even past Abraham to Adam, who is also said to
be "son of God" [*tou theou*] (v 38). Coming where it does in
the story, the genealogy has the effect of indicating that
Jesus' sonship, besides being divine in the direct way
(conceived by the Spirit of God), is also a sonship that is in
full solidarity with Israel (son of David and son of
Abraham); even more, it is a sonship in solidarity with the
total human family—as son of that first son of God, Adam.

Jesus' sonship receives further elaboration in the narrative
which follows the genealogy, the testing in the desert (4:1-
13). The devil there expresses the first and last temptations
with the phrase, "If you are the Son of God . . . ." The
nature of the testing, the context in Deuteronomy from
which Jesus' answers come, and the OT identification of
Israel collectively as "son" (Ex 4:22; Hos 11:1) all point to
the most common interpretation that this account presents
Jesus as the representive of the true Israel reversing with his
obedience the disobedience of Israel of old.

There is very likely a new-Adam typology also at work
here.[2] After all, the words immediately preceding this
account are the end of the genealogy, "son of Adam, son of
God." Lk 4:1-13 then proceeds to demonstrate how *this* son
of Adam proves to be a true son of God by his obedience to
God.[3] Other-wordly voices repeat the title at 8:28; 9:35; and

---

[2] See J. Neyrey, *The Passion According to Luke* (New York: Paulist, 1985), esp. pp.
164-175.

[3] *Pace* J. Fitzmyer (*Luke I-IX*, 512), there is no reason to deny the possibility of
Luke's adding an Adamic resonance to a tradition whose pre-Lukan point may have
been the Jesus/Israel parallel.

it is used for the last time in the narrative, in a climactic way, at the trial of Jesus before the Sanhedrin: "And they all said, 'Are you the Son of God, then?' And he said to them, 'You say that I am'" (22:70). For our purpose it is enough to note that the Jesus who speaks the beatitudes has been introduced to the reader as Son of God in a sense that transcends the merely messianic.

B) SON OF DAVID

Gabriel also announces Jesus as son and heir of David (1:32). The Davidic lineage of his legal father Joseph is thrice affirmed (1:27; 2:4; 3:31). The Benedictus of Zechariah heralds Jesus as a horn of salvation raised up in the house of God's servant David (1:69). These references underscore Jesus' messianic credentials. The remainder of the story of Luke-Acts makes it clear that though Jesus fulfills the role of Messiah, he also transcends that role. For the blind man of Jericho first addresses Jesus twice as Son of David (18:38-39) but then, at the actual encounter, he pointly calls him *Lord (kyrie)*. Similarly, teaching in the temple near the end, Jesus raises the issue of Davidic sonship one last time (20:41,42,44) only to imply that "son of David" is transcended by the title "Lord." Indeed, when Jesus is announced as fulfilling his credentials as son and heir of David in Acts, it is as risen Lord (Acts 2:30-36).

C) SAVIOR AND CHRIST

The angelic announcement to the shepherds, "For to you is born this day in the city of David a Savior who is Christ the Lord" (2:11), is the richest titular statement made about Jesus in the infancy narrative. "Savior" is first used of Yahweh (1:47, "God my Savior" in the opening line of the Magnificat) and then applied to Jesus three times in Luke-Acts: here, and in two speeches in Acts 5:31 and 13:23.

Christ (Greek for "Anointed One"; "Messiah" in Hebrew) is introduced for the first time in Luke here in this Christmas message. Luke's introduction of Simeon says that "it had been revealed to him by the Holy Spirit that he should not see death before he had seen the Lord's Christ" (2:26). Then he comes into the temple to take up the child Jesus and sing his Nunc Dimittis. When John the Baptist makes his debut, Luke says that people questioned in their hearts concerning John, "whether perhaps he were the Christ" (3:15). Finally, at the end of the day of healing at Capernaum, it is said that Jesus rebuked the demons and would not allow them to speak, because they knew that he was the Christ (4:41). It is, then, both as the expected Messiah ("the Lord's Christ," 2:26) and as one who is more than the expected Messiah ("Christ the Lord," 2:11) that Jesus speaks the beatitudes. Luke uses all the titles with creative flexibility, perhaps none more creatively than Christ, Anointed One, as a study of his handling of Jesus' role as Prophet will illustrate.

D) PROPHET

Apart from the gospels themselves, the category of prophet has been little used by Christian tradition for interpreting the person of Jesus. This is understandable. For in the light of the full development of the doctrines of incarnation and trinity, the category of prophet appears irrelevant to Christology. It was not thus for Matthew, Mark, Luke and John. Indeed, the biblical notion of prophet was perhaps the most important title and "model" for Jesus in the introductory section of the Gospel of Luke.

The Baptist's prophetic role (see 1:15, 17, 76; 3:1-3; 7:26) is a mere sketch of that role as Jesus fills (and transcends) it. The first allusion to Jesus' prophetic role is Simeon's naming the newborn child "a light for the revelation to the Gentiles," a phrase used of the Isaian Servant of Yahweh in Is 42:6 and 49:6.[4] That connection having been established, the reader is prepared to hear an allusion to the opening line of the first Servant Song (Is 42:1) in the final words of the voice from

---

[4]Stephen Farris (*The Hymns of Luke's Infancy Narratives* [JSNT Supplement Series 9; Sheffield: JSOT Press 1985] 150) notes that the curious Greek phrase *phōs ethnōn* (literally, "light of the gentiles") is exactly the phrase which appears in the LXX at Is 42:6 and 49:6).

heaven at the Jordan, "with thee I am well pleased."

What is delicately foreshadowed in the early chapters comes to vivid expression in Lk 4:16-44 (the beginning of Jesus' public ministry in Nazareth and Capernaum). Here Jesus' identity is portrayed in a variety of ways:

1. In this first episode of this public ministry in his home town, Jesus explicitly identifies himself with the prophetic figure of Is 61:1-2.

2. He is identifying the time and the audience with those implicit in the Isaian passage. That is, when he says, "Today this scripture has been fulfilled in your hearing" [literally, "in your *ears*"; whether they *hear* with those ears is another question], he is saying that the end-time visitation of God indicated by the Isaian language of proclaiming good news, is happening now. Moreover, since it is in *their* ears that this scripture has been fulfilled, *they* are being addressed as "poor," "captive," "blind," "oppressed." Whether they recognize themselves as such is a separate question.

3. Besides identifying himself with the prophetic figure of Is 61:1; 58:6, he applies to this situation the proverb about no prophet being acceptable in his own country.

4. He goes on to compare his mission and its reception to the classical prophets Elijah and Elisha.

5. After the association of Jesus with the wonder-working prophets fresh in our minds, what follows in chapter 4 is easily understood as prophetic *action*. In the episode in the Capernaum synagogue which follows, Jesus' authority (*exousia*) finds expression in both his teaching (4:31) and his deliverance from demonic oppression (v 36). Both the teaching and the cure are referred to in Luke's version of the account as a function of the prophet's *word* (Lk 4:32, 36).[5] Since, in Luke's story line, Jesus

---

[5]Luke's retelling of Mk 1:22-28 is interesting. Luke enhances Jesus' authority by showing that Jesus' command to the demon to be silent was successful (in Mk 1:26 the demon *dis*obeys by crying out). Second, Luke heightens the unity of Jesus' teaching and healing (already present in Mark's reference to the deliverence as the sign of "A new teaching," Mk 1:27)[6]by referring to both operations as a function of Jesus' "word" [*logos*]: " ... and they were astonished at his teaching, for his *word* was with authority" (Lk 4:32) and, in response to the deliverance, "What is this *word?* For with authority and power he commands the unclean spirits and they come out" (v 36b).

has not yet called any disciples, he enters Simon's house alone and cures Simon's mother-in-law from a high fever, not with a touch (as in Mk 1:31), but with the same authority of *word* (4:39) with which he rebuked the demon oppressing the man in the synagogue. Finally, in the description of the healing of the sick at evening, Luke further affirms Jesus' authority of word and work (1) by saying that "*all* those who had any that were sick . . . brought them to him" and that he "laid his hands on *every one of them* and healed them" and (2) by again *rebuking* the demons for saying, "You are the Son of God."

6. The two verses (Lk 4:42-43) describing Jesus' departure from Capernaum present decisive clues regarding Luke's intention in his presentation of Jesus as prophet. When Jesus departs for a lonely place, it is not (as in Mk 1:36) Simon and other disciples who approach Jesus, but *people* [*hoi ochloi*], since in Luke's story line, Jesus has not yet called any disciples. To those who would restrain his moving on, Jesus says, "I must preach the good news of the kingdom of God [*euangelisasthai me dei tēn basileian tou theou*] to the other cities also; for I was sent [*apestalēn*] for this purpose. And he was preaching [*ēnkeryssōn*] in the synagogues of Judea."

This way of completing chapter four is significant for two reasons. First, it is the second in a long series of statements in which divine purpose is underscored by the Greek word *dei* ("it is necessary"), of which the first was "Did you not know that I *must* be in my Father's house?" (2:49) And the next such statement will be 9:22, the first passion prediction, ("The Son of man *must* suffer many things, and be rejected . . .").[6] Second, the phrase "to preach the good news" (or "to bring glad tidings") translates a single verb in the Greek, *euangelisasthai*. A favorite in Luke's vocabulary (occurring 25x in Luke-Acts and only one other place in the four gospels, Mt 11:15, an allusion to Is 61:6), it is rare in the LXX, with Luke's favorite prophet, Isaiah, using the word six times (of the 22 OT instances)—Is 49:9 (twice) 52:7 (twice) 60:6; 61:1. Two of these texts are worth quoting in full:

---

[6]Other important places where Luke uses *dei* are Lk 2:49; 9:22; 12:12; 13:14, 16, 33; 15:32; 17:25; 18:1; 19:5; 21:9; 22:7, 37; 24:7, 26, 44; Acts 1:16, 21; 3:21; 4:14; 5:29; 9:6, 16; plus sixteen more places in Acts.

> Go up into a high mountain,
>> Zion, herald of glad tidings [*ho euangelizomenos*].
> Lift up your voice with strength
>> Jerusalem, herald of good news [*ho euangelizomenos*]
> Lift up; fear not,
>> Say to the cities of Judah, "behold your God."[7]
> (Is 40:9)

> How beautiful upon the mountains
> are the feet of him who brings glad tidings
> Announcing peace, bearing good news,
>> announcing salvation, and saying to Zion,
>> "Your God is King!"[8] (Is 52:7)

The most important text, of course, is Is 61:1, which was quoted as the text read in Lk 4:18-19.

In the introductory chapters of Luke, *euangelizomai* describes Gabriel's announcing to Zechariah (1:19), the angel of the Lord's communication to the shepherds (2:10), and John the Baptist's exhortations in the wilderness (3:18). Next it occurs in the quotation of Is 61 at 4:18, and then in the summary verse under consideration. It is reasonable to conclude that Luke uses the word in the spirit of Isaiah and that the angelic messengers and the Baptist are said to "bring glad tidings" because they herald the new age, indeed, the kingdom of God in the sense of Isaiah, especially Is 61. The presence of *apestalēn* and *kēryssōn* in these final verses of Lk 4 also echo Is 61 and suggest that that passage is the background against which Luke wants the reader to hear *euangelisasthai*.

Further, we note that v 43 contains Luke's first use of the expression "kingdom of God." Presumably, we can expect a responsible writer to provide the appropriate context for understanding key concepts. Since an Isaian context has been provided for *euangelizomai*, we do well to attend to the Isaian

---

[7]For this last statement, the targum of Isaiah reads, "The kingdom of your God revealed" (Bruce D. Chilton [ed.] *The Isaiah Targum* [The Aramaic Bible, vol. 11: Wilmington DE: Michael Glazier, 1987] 77).

[8]Again, the Isaiah targum has, "The kingdom of your God is revealed" (Chilton, *Isaiah Targum*, 102).

meaning of kingdom of God, which is nothing less than the
end-time salvation of God.[9] In what sense is the salvation of
God to be understood in Lk 4? How has Jesus "heralded the
Kingdom of God" (4:43)? It would seem to be the teaching
and healing that has just been described in the previous thirty-
one verses. The debut in the synagogue at Nazareth and the
response of the people (4:16-30) announce Jesus as eschatological prophet and anticipate his ministry at Capernaum (v
23). Then the day and evening of healing at Capernaum (vv
31-41) show Jesus exercizing that prophetic authority in word
and deed. The demonic confession that Jesus is "Son of God,"
equated by Luke with being called "the Christ," suggests that
the quotation from Is 61, "he has *anointed* [*echrisen,*, lit.,
"christed"] me," is meant to interpret the meaning of Christ
(Anointed One; Messiah, in Hebrew) as referring, at least in
part, to Jesus as anointed end-time prophet.[10] That is, along
with indicating Jesus' fulfillment of the role of expected royal
son of David, the title "Christ" means equally, and perhaps
more importantly for Luke, the Prophet who makes available
the expected Kingdom of God through his teaching and
healing.

This whole section (4:14-44) also looks backward to the
manifestation of the Holy Spirit at the Jordan (3:21-22). For
the words, "The Spirit of the Lord is upon me," remind the
reader of the scene in the previous chapter where the Holy
Spirit descended upon Jesus in bodily form and the voice from
heaven spoke to him in words alluding the Isaian figure of the
Servant of Yahweh.[11] That Luke understands the Is 61 quotation as interpreting the baptism episode is confirmed in the
speech of Peter in Acts 10:36-38:

---

[9]See Bruce D. Chilton (*God in Strength: Jesus' Announcement of the Kingdom*
[SNTU Series B, Band 1; Freistadt: F. Ploechl, 1979]) who finds in the targum of
Isaiah the matrix for Jesus' understanding of the kingdom of God, which he interprets
as "God come in strength" or "the self-manifestation of God."

[10]This flexible working with the verbal root of *Christos* in the Greek verb *chriein* is
evident in Acts 4:24-28, where the title *Christos* in the quoted Ps 2 is interpreted as a
reference to the divine anointing in v 27: "Jesus, whom you anointed [*hon echrisas*]."

[11]As for the relationship between the prophetic figure of Is 61 to the Servant figure
in Second Isaiah, see the literature mentioned in notes 12 and 14 of Part One.

"You know the word which [God] sent to Israel, preaching good news [*euangelizomenos*] of peace by Jesus Christ (he is Lord of all), the word which was proclaimed throughout all Judea, beginning from Galilee after the baptism which John preached: how God anointed [*echrisen*] Jesus of Nazareth with the Holy Spirit and with power; how he went about doing good and healing all that were oppressed by the devil, for God was with him."

This constitutes a complete summary of Lk 3:21-4:44. It is as this anointed end-time Prophet (who, again, breaks the prophetic mold of Jewish expectation) that Jesus comes forward and speaks the beatitudes.

E) THE SON OF MAN

There remains the section 5:1-6:19. What further contribution do these episodes make in the introduction of Jesus as speaker of the Lucan beatitudes? In this stretch of the narrative we meet Jesus in a variety of roles and capacities. He continues to act with prophetic authority, which in this portion of the narrative begins to be associated with the title Son of Man. Whereas Mark presented Jesus as calling the first disciples early in this story (Mk 1:16-20), Luke waits until he has shown Jesus as the rejected prophet who continues to teach and heal (a pattern which will be the story of the church in Acts) and then has Jesus call Peter and the brothers Zebedee. In this scene Jesus preaches the "word of God" to large crowds, give a fruitful command (in a hopeless situation) regarding fishing, is addressed as "Master" and then "Lord" by Simon, and finally calls Simon to "catch" people.

Jesus heals a leper with a touch and a word (5:13) and, when great multitudes gather to hear and be healed, he withdraws to the wilderness for prayer.

Next, following Mark's sequence, Luke gives us a cluster of five controversies focused on healing and eating (5:17-6:11):

1) the cure of the paralytic, which shows that Jesus is the Son of man who has "authority on earth" not only to cure but to forgive sins;

2) the call of Levi and the subsequent feast with tax collectors and sinners, where Jesus is a "physician" who ministers to the socially outcast by calling them to repentance in the context of table fellowship;

3) the discussion of fasting (which Luke makes part of the banquet scene at Levi's), where Jesus uses imagery of bridegroom, new garment, and new wine to underscore the newness he is introducing as eschatological prophet;

4) the controversy about plucking grain on the sabbath, in which Jesus asserts that he is the Son of Man who is even Lord of the sabbath;

5) and the sabbath healing of a man with a withered hand, where Jesus asserts his Lordship of the sabbath by confronting his adversaries on the real level of their opposition: they are bent on destroying life, he on saving life.

When Jesus withdraws to spend a night praying to God and then proceeds to choose from his disciples a group of twelve whom he calls "apostles" (*apostolous*, literally "sent ones"), he does this as the prophet who has been *sent* (in the manner described by Is 61) to heal, preach, suffer rejection; he is, moreover one who has been called Lord, Savior, Son of God, Son of Man, and Christ—i.e. Anointed One in a double sense, messianic Son of David and chosen eschatological Prophet.

When Jesus comes down from the mountain to take his stand on a level place, Luke strikes one more note to highlight the fact that Jesus is present as a prophetic agent of God: "And all the crowd sought to touch him for *power [dynamis] came forth from him and healed them all.*" The preceding chapters have taught us how to hear that description. The angel had said that John would go before the Lord "in the spirit and *dynamis* of Elijah," thereby associating spirit and power with the OT prophetic tradition. But Jesus would follow through and transcend that tradition by being conceived in the Holy Spirit and the *dynamis* of the Most High (1:35). After the temptations in the wilderness, he returns "in the *dynamis* of the Spirit" (4:14). In response to the deliverance in the synagogue, bystanders remark, "With authority and *dynamis* he commands the unclean spirits" (4:36). And, most pertinently, shortly after another recess for prayer in the wilderness (5:16), Jesus is teaching in a house, and Luke says, "the *dynamis* of the Lord was with him to heal." And now here, in the setting of the Sermon of the Plain, after another time of intense prayer to God, it is said that *dynamis* is with him to heal. The reader has been prepared to understand that that means Jesus is operating as the Son of God functioning as end-time Prophet with the authority of the apocalyptic Son of Man.

II. To Whom is He Talking?

Both Luke and Matthew exercise considerable care in crafting the audience and setting of the Great Sermon to which the beatitudes provide the introduction. Since our understanding of the beatitudes is profoundly conditioned by our assumptions about the addressees, it is crucial that we take seriously the evangelists' portrayal of setting and audience.

A) THE IMMEDIATE SETTING: LK 6:17-20

Luke describes the immediate audience of the Great Sermon in this way:

> And he came down with them and stood on a level place, with a great crowd of his disciples and a great multitude of the people from all Judea and Jerusalem and the seacoast of Tyre and Sidon, where those who were troubled with unclean spirits were cured. And all the crowd sought to touch him, for power came forth from him and healed them all.

A comparison with Mark shows that Luke has omitted Mark's description of the massive scene of gathering and healing (Mk 3:7-12) which precedes the call of the twelve (Mk 3:13-19) and remodels it to provide the setting for the Sermon on the Plain. It should be noted that already in Mark the gathering is an idealized scene, picturing a crowd spontaneously drawn by hearsay from distances of forty, sixty, and even a hundred miles away (Idumea). Note that the scene is not a *summary*, as some commentators call it, for it does not summarize what occurs over an extended period of ministry but rather pictures (with aorist verbs) a one-time gathering. (North Americans over 40 might picture it as an instant "Woodstock" without benefit of modern means of communication and travel.)

Those with whom Jesus "came down" are presumably the "disciples" who had been on the mountain with him (v13) and the twelve specially chosen from among them to be apostles (vv 13-16). The "great crowd of his disciples" (v 17) is an even larger circle of those who follow Jesus. In Acts "disciples" [*mathētai*] is the name by which all believers are called. That they are called a "*great crowd* of disciples" is surprising, inasmuch as we have met only a handful up to this point; one would have guessed little more than twelve. "A great multitude of the people [*plēthos poly tou laou*] from all Judea and Jerusalem and the seacoast of Tyre and Sidon" broadens the audience enormously. "Judea" here seems to be used in the generic sense of all Palestine (as in, e.g., 4:44; 7:17; 23:5). A great multitude from *all* Judea, and drawing even from the farther reaches of Tyre and Sidon, gives us a full representation of Israel. Indeed, it is a crowd that evokes the full Old Testament resonance of the word "the people"—*ho laos*—a resonance Luke has evoked before (1:10, 17, 21, 68, 77; 2:10, 31, 32; 3:15, 18, 21). And when Luke resumes the narrative after the speech, he puts it this way, "After he had ended all his sayings in the hearing of *the people* he entered Capernaum" (7:1). Consequently, it is the people, understood as representing all Israel, who constitute Jesus' audience.

B) THE GATHERING OF END-TIME ISRAEL

From the very first scenes of the Third Gospel, the atmosphere has been that of an expectant Israel receiving divine communication. A righteous temple priest, Zechariah, focusing the worship of "the whole multitude of the people," hears a message from the apocalyptic angel Gabriel that his wife shall give birth to a prophet who will call Israel to a renewal, a conversion, "to make ready for the Lord a people prepared: (1:17). And the focus on divine visitation of an expectant people continues. The child to be born of Mary will "reign

over the house of Jacob forever" (1:33). In the hymn of the
Benedictus, Mary celebrates her pregnancy as a fulfillment of
divine promise to the ancestors: "He has upheld Israel his
servant, ever mindful of his mercy; even as he promised our
fathers, promised Abraham and his descendants forever"
(1:53-55). In a similar mode, Zechariah, on the occasion of the
circumcision of John the Baptist, celebrates Jesus as a divine
visitation and ransoming of his people (1:67) and the emer-
gence of the mature John the Baptist, is described as "the day
of his manifestation *to Israel*" (1:80). The angelic announcement to the shepherds speaks of "a great joy which will come
to *all the people*" (2:10). As Simeon is introduced to sing his
Nunc Dimittis, he is introduced as awaiting "the consolation
of Israel" (2:25). His canticle calls the newborn Jesus "a light
for revelation to the Gentiles, and for thy people *Israel*" (2:32)
and, moreover, a child "set for the fall and rising of many in
Israel" (v 34). He is joined by the prophetess Anna who was
speaking of Jesus to "all who were looking for redemption of
Jerusalem" (where, in familiar OT convention, the capital
surely stands for the nation as a whole). It is to a representative
gathering of end-time Israel that Jesus speaks the Sermon on
the Plain.

"The great crowd of disciples," then, comprises a subgroup
of the gathered *laos*, and the Twelve, of course, are a subset
within the crowd of disciples. In his use of the term *disciples*
for a larger group of followers of Jesus, Luke differs from
Matthew and Mark, who *equate* the disciples and the twelve
(and they portray broader Christian discipleship through the
symbol of the twelve). Inasmuch as the narrative thus far has
introduced only a handful of disciples (Simon, the Zebedee
brothers, Levi, and finally the twelve-plus mentioned in 6:12-
16), the reader is unprepared for the "great crowd of his
disciples" mentioned here. Indeed, for the remainder of the
Third Gospel, the term "disciples" when used of a group
appears to be confined to the inner circle of the twelve, the
single exception being 19:37, where the group with Jesus during
the messianic entry into Jerusalem is called "the multitude of
the disciples." This last group voices the climactic choral
response to the whole public ministry of Jesus up to this point:
they "rejoice and praise God with a loud voice for all the

mighty works that they had seen, saying 'Blessed is the king . . .'" Both of these exceptional descriptions of a great crowd of disciples call attention to themselves and appear to be Luke's preview of the post-Easter community—what scholars call a "proleptic reference."[12]

The motive of the crowds is typical of Luke's description of crowds coming to Jesus: they came *to hear* him and *to be healed of their diseases* (v 17). In the previous chapter, following the healing of the leper, "great multitudes gathered *to hear* and *to be healed of their infirmities*" (5:17). Luke emphasizes that for the end-time Prophet healing and teaching go together (see also 9:2-11 and 10:9).

When Luke introduces the Sermon on the Plain, then, with the words, "And he lifted up his eyes on his disciples, and said . . . ," the *immediate* audience is the many followers implied by the word "disciples," including the subset of the recently chosen twelve apostles; but Jesus addresses as well the less committed members of this ingathering of the people of Israel, in whose *hearing* the words are spoken (6:17 and 7:1).[13]

C) ARE THE ADDRESSEES OF THE WOES PRESENT?

Verses 24-26 represent a definite shift. After the four beatitudes, Jesus says, "But woe to you that are rich, for you have

---

[12]Another example of Luke's stylized enhancement of Jesus' audience occurs in the scene of the healing of the paralytic at 5:17b, where Luke takes Mark's mention of "some of the scribes" (Mk 2:6) in the middle of the story and incorporates the detail in expanded form as part of the setting: "there were Pharisees and teachers of the law sitting by, *who had come from every village of Galilee and Judea and from Jerusalem* ___ "—a considerable assembly for the narrow confines of one of the small dwellings whose dimensions can be inferred from the first-century remains currently coming to light at the dig at Capernaum. This scene, too, appears to be proleptic, foreshadowing the full resistance Jesus would meet at the end of his public life as well as the resistance to be met by the church of Acts.

[13]That Luke can picture Jesus addressing the disciples in the hearing of the people is illustrated by his introduction at 20:45: "and in the hearing of all the people he said to his disciples, 'Beware of the scribes . . . '"

received your consolation."[14] Then, after the three woes which
follow, the words of the speech continue at v 27, "*But I say to
you that hear,* Love your enemies..." Some commentators
take this transition as an indication that Luke realized that the
woes would not apply to the disciples and therefore makes an
awkward transition to suggest that those woes would only
apply to resisters of Jesus who would not be numbered among
the audience of disciples. I suggest that Luke is more coherent
than that. We have already seen that the author imagines a
larger audience of the people listening in on his address to the
disciples. A further consideration is Luke's thematic emphasis
on the distinction between merely hearing and really *listening*
obediently. Introducing the parable of the two builders which
winds up the speech, Jesus says, "Every one who comes to me
and *hears* my words and does them, I will show you what he is
like ... " (v 47). This theme appears in Luke's redaction of the
interpretation of the parable of The Sower, which introduces a
distinction between hearing and believing only hinted at in
Mark's version. See 8:12-13, 18, and the climax, v 21: "My
mother and my brothers are those *who hear the word of God
and do it."* Given this way of speaking of true hearing as
obedience to the word of God, it is clear that the woes are
addressed to those in the gathering of the people who resist the
invitation to discipleship.

III. What Time Is It?

One of the insights that emerge from our look at the speaker
and his audience, as introduced in the early chapters of Luke,
is that our author is preoccupied with time, the particular
moment in sacred history which the advent of Jesus initiates.
The gradually emerging picture of Jesus as end-time Prophet
addressing ingathered end-time Israel raises a question: Are
there further clues in Luke-Acts which suggest that the Third

---

[14]The second-person form of address of this woe is even stronger than that of the
beatitudes, for the Greek text explicitly says "you" (plural) [*hymin*] in the first, second
and fourth woes, whereas it is missing in Luke's beatitudes ("Blessed: the poor") and
mentioned only in the second element ("for *yours* is the kingdom of God").

Evangelist is presenting the inbreaking of the expected eschatological era? There are. A few of the clues follow:

1. The appearance of Gabriel, last seen in the biblical canon in Dan 8:16ff and 9:21ff, evokes end-time associations, for the vision of the seventy weeks of years points to a time when "everlasting justice will be introduced, vision and prophecy will be ratified".[15]

2. The coming of Jesus is identified with Zechariah's expectation of "the consolation of Israel" (2:25) and others' expectation of "the deliverance of Jerusalem" (2:35)—phrases which evoke end-time salvation.

3. The quotation of Is 61:1 (and 58:6) is said to be fulfilled in the listeners' ear *today* (*sēmeron*, 4:21), meaning that the future salvation envisioned in Trito-Isaiah is fulfilled especially in Jesus' public ministry. See, too, the "today" sayings at 5:26; 19:5,9; and 23:43.

4. The question of John the Baptist's embassy, "Are you he who is to come, or shall we look for another?" (7:19), is answered by Jesus by way of allusion to several salvation oracles in Isaiah (29:18-19; 35:5-6; 61:1), confirming what we had seen in our interpretation of the day of healing at Capernaum, namely, that Jesus' healings are evidence of the presence of the end-time kingdom of God.

5. In response to the charge that he casts out demons by Beelzebul, Jesus speaks in language which interprets his deliverance ministry as a new exodus and the manifestation of the Reign of God: "But if it is by the finger of God that I cast out demons, then the kingdom of God has come upon you" (11:20).[16]

6. The presence of the kingdom is put even more strongly in the answer to the Pharisees' question in 17:20: "The kingdom of God is in the midst of you."

---

[15]R. Brown discusses this Danielic background in *The Birth of the Messiah* (Garden City, NY: Doubleday, 1977) 270-271.

[16]"Finger of God" is an allusion to Ex 8:19, where the Pharaoh's court magicians, unable to replicate the gnat plague say, "The finger of God [i.e. Yahweh of the Hebrews] is here." The verb describing the arrival of the Kingdom of God here is *ephthasen*, a word used only here (and in the Matthean parallel 12:28) in the synoptics, meaning "has arrived," as for example, in LXX Dan 7:13,21.

7. There is evidence that Luke understands the story of Jesus and the beginnings of the Jerusalem church to be two phases in the inauguration of the end-time manifestation of the Kingdom of God, with Jesus' preaching and healing being the first phase and the Pentecostal birth of the church being the second phase. The establishment of the church through the outpouring of the Holy Spirit on Pentecost is seen as the fulfillment of the hope for an end-time restoration of Israel. This was forecast by Jesus' words at the Last Supper ("as my Father appointed a kingdom for me, so do I appoint for you that you may eat and drink at my table in my kingdom, and sit on thrones judging the twelve tribes of Israel" (22:29-30). This commission is implemented in the early chapters of Acts, where the apostles, their number carefully restored to Twelve, preside over an ingathering of Israelites from all corners of the diaspora and interpret the happenings of Easter and Pentecost with such words as Acts 2:17, 30-36, 3:24 ("and all the prophets who have spoken, from Samuel and those who came afterwards, also proclaimed *these days*"), and 15:16-18 (the restoration of the "fallen dwelling of David" [Israel] precedes the mission to the gentiles).[17]

8. Luke's flexible treatment of the kingdom of God embraces both the strong manifestation of that kingdom in the ministry of Jesus and the church and an expectation of future fulfillment. The sense of *present* manifestation shows in 4:43; 8:1, 10; 9:2,11; 9:27; 10:9; 11:20; 12:31; 16:16 ("everyone is pressed to enter it"); 17:20-21 ("in your midst"). The hope for the kingdom's definitive fulfillment in the *future* is carried by such statements as 11:2 ("thy kingdom come"), 13:28-29 (end-time banquet); 14:15; 19:11; and 21:31.

Our interpretation of the end-time atmosphere of the setting of the Sermon on the Plain is, therefore, consistent with the rest of Luke's scheme of salvation history.

---

[17]This interpretation of Luke 22:28-30 is well argued by Jacob Jervell, *Luke and the People of God* (Minneapolis: Augsburg, 1972), esp. pp. 75-112, "The Twelve on Israel's Thrones."

IV. Who are the Poor and the Rich in Luke's Beatitudes and Woes?

Since "rich" and "poor" carry powerful social and emotional connotations in contemporary North American English, the impulse is strong to impose on these biblical words our own interpretations and agendas. Consequently, it is important that we take pains to hear what "rich" and "poor" mean for Luke.

A) THE POOR

1. Those called ptōchos ("poor, afflicted, oppressed")

What does Luke mean by *hoi ptōchoi* (the poor)? The lexicographers note that first-century Greek used two words that we might translate "poor" in English, *penēs*, which denoted a person who had employment but was of slender means, and *ptōchos*, "begging, dependent on others for support."[18] The word *ptōchos* also carried connotations from the Greek translation of the Old Testament (the Septuagint) where, especially in the Psalms and Isaiah, it often referred to those who are so oppressed that they are in special need of God's help.

Within those dictionary possibilities, how in fact does the Third Evangelist use the word? Only two *individuals* are termed *ptōchos* in Luke, the widow who contributed all that she had in the form of two copper coins (21:3) and the beggar Lazarus in the parable of The Rich Man and Lazarus (16:20, 22). The seven other references in Luke (there are none in Acts) are in the generic plural. They include those to whom the rich man is invited to give the worth of all his property (18:22), those to whom Zacchaeus resolves to give half his goods (19:8), and those among Jesus' preferred banquet guest

---

[18]BAGD, 728. F. Hauck ("Ptōchos," *TDNT*, 6 [1968] 886) notes that *ptōchos* is etymologically related to *ptōssein*, "to bow down timidly," and says, further, "whereas *penēs* denotes one who has to earn his living because he has no property, *ptōchos* denotes the complete destitution which forces the poor to seek the help of others by begging."

list (14:13,21). Important for us in our search for Luke's specific meaning for "poor" as he uses it in his first beatitude is the fact that this saying at 6:20 stands between two other uses of *ptōchoi,* the quotation of Is 61:1 at 4:18 and the allusion to that same seminal Isaian passage at 7:22. It would seem that our author has provided in his references to Isaiah 61 the biblical context in which he would have us understand *hoi ptōchoi* in the beatitude.

2. Isaiah's meaning for "poor"

We have good reason to believe that Luke uses the language of Isaiah with an appreciative sensitivity to the broader context of the passages he chooses to quote or allude to. We have already had occasion to discuss his use of the Servant of Yahweh imagery to interpret Jesus and his employment of *euangelizomai* with the Isaianic connotation. [19] In the primary passage, Is 61 as quoted at Lk 4:18, *ptōchoi* translates *anawim* ("the lowly" in the NAB) and stands in parallel with "the broken hearted," "the captives" ("the blind" in the LXX version which Luke quotes at 4:18), "the oppressed" (added from Is 58:6 in Lk 4:18), and "the mourning." In this setting, it is clear that the *ptōchoi* are not some group or class to be distinguished from the broken hearted, the captive, and the mourning; rather *ptōchoi* is a term paralleling the others in a description of the faithful in post-exilic Israel who still, even after the return, yearn for the definitive saving intervention of God. Is 61:1-3 is an application of the Servant-of-Yahweh imagery from Second Isaiah to the prophetic community of Trito-Isaiah. This prophetic figure is pictured as addressing the larger community of Judah (representing the full twelve-tribe Israel of old) and announcing to them that hoped-for salvation. In the Greek version of Second and Third Isaiah (i.e., chaps. 40-66), *ptōchoi* are the people as a whole in need of salvation from their God (see 41:17 and 61:1). [20] The imagery of hungering and weeping, too, employs conventional OT language for

---

[19]See D. P. Seccombe, "Luke and Isaiah, "*NTS* 27 (1981) 252-259.

[20]D. P. Seccombe, (*Possessions and the Poor in Luke-Acts* [SNTU Series B, Vol 6; Linz, Austria: Harrachstrasse 7, 1982], pp. 24-69) developes this in some detail.

describing the people as a whole in need of help from their God (see the beatitudes in Ps 34:6-10; Ps 146:5-7; and Is 26:6; 40:28-30; 49:10; 55:1-3).

3. *The economically poor who are not called* ptōchoi

Besides those indigent actually described by the adjective *ptōchoi*, there are others who, although the word is not associated with them, surely share in the lot of the indigent: the needy to whom John the Baptist exhorts the crowds to give their extra tunic or their surplus food (3:10); those reduced to borrowing and stealing (6:29-30); the sick, maimed, blind, lame who if they were not supported by an extended family, were reduced to begging (cf. the blind beggar of Jericho, 18:35-43 [alias Bartimeaus, in Mk 10] and the man born lame in Acts 3); widows without that culture's necessary male support (e.g. the widow of Nain [7:11-12], the widow in the parable of The Corrupt Judge [18:1-8], and the Greek-speaking widows of the Jerusalem Christian community [Acts 6:1-6]); and those among the Jerusalem community whose needs were met through benefactions distributed by the apostles (Acts 4:34-35). Are these needy people the kind of people congratulated by the first beatitude? Indirectly, yes. Each of these people has been touched in some way by the end-time manifestation of God's power. Even the poor of the parables represent such beneficiaries of the kingdom.

4. *Social outcasts*

Then there are those who are poor because they are social outcasts. Since any physical infirmity was considered a divine judgment for one's sinfulness, the sick, the crippled, the blind, the lame, the demonized, the infertile, were all in some sense socially outcast. Elizabeth, who suffered the shame of being childless (1:7,25), is the first such person we meet in Luke (and she is the first blessed by divine intervention when God removes that curse through the conception of John). Every healing or deliverance which follows would also have been perceived as a similar act of divine removal of a curse.

Others were socially outcast because they were members of a profession or trade proscribed as unclean, e.g. tax collectors, shepherds, prostitutes, and those considered "sinners" because their following of the Law was habitually delinquent. That shepherds were the first recipients of the good news of the Savior's birth was exemplification of "good news to the poor." Jesus' hosting of tax-collectors and sinners was more of the same. Thus the healed sick person in the setting of the Sermon can be called fortunate poor because with Jesus' presence the sick have received the healing they sought.

5. *Those poor in the Isaian sense*

Then there are those who show themselves to be poor in the Isaian sense (of knowing their need for God) even though nothing is said of their financial or social need: e.g. Zechariah (whose moment of disbelief serves to highlight his otherwise obedient righteousness), the prophetess Anna, Simeon, Mary the mother of Jesus, and Zacchaeus. The teaching of Jesus on the occasion of the blessing of infants at Lk 18:15-17 may be our best commentary on the essence of the poverty of the first beatitude. "Let the children come to me, and do not hinder them; for to such belongs the kingdom of God. Truly, I say to you, whoever does not receive the kingdom of God like a child shall not enter it."

6. *Excursus: Where do Jesus and the disciples fit among the poor?*

Although popular piety has understood some features of Jesus' birth and infancy (no room in the inn, the manger-crib, the simpler offering of the doves at the presentation) as signs of an origin in poverty, it seems more accurate to acknowledge that the life-style of a craftsman (*tekton*)[21], while not wealthy, was not indigent. What is more pertinent is Jesus' choice, during his public ministry, to minister to the sick and demonized, to share table fellowship with the tax collectors and sinners, and to live as the Son of man who "has nowhere to lay his head" (9:58). Similarly, the group of apostles included the brothers Zebedee (whose fishing business was properous

---

[21]A *tekton* was a carpenter, wood-worker, builder according to BAGD, 809. Jesus in Mt 13:55 is called "the son of the *tekton*" and in Mk 6:3 "the *tekton*."

enough to include hired help). The centurion of Capernaum, who exemplified for Jesus the faith proper to true Israelites, was wealthy enough to sponsor the building of the local synagogue. At least some of the women who traveled with and served Jesus and the Twelve came from the privileged (e.g. Joanna, the wife of Herod's steward, Lk 8:3). Zacchaeus was a *chief* toll collector who manifests discipleship by giving up *half* his goods.

On the other hand, the core dozen are said to have left everything to follow Jesus. What is more, they (in chapter 9) and, after them, the seventy-two (Lk 10), are sent on the extension of his prophetic mission and they are charged to follow a strikingly spare life style. The apostolic equipment includes (combining here the list for the twelve and the list for the seventy-two) no money, no bag, no extra tunic, no sandals, no staff, no bread, and they are to engage in no road-side greetings. They are to move from town to town, preaching and healing, absorbing the hospitality (food, drink, and shelter) of whatever household receives them. And the rationale for accepting the hospitality is, "the laborer is worth his wages" (10:7, a development of the harvest image used in v 2). This is something other than solidarity with the poor. The needy would not move from town to town. And no one traveled the threatening, rocky Palestinian roads without sandals and staff. Such behavior is not poverty but prophetic strategy. Indeed, after the sending of Twelve, Luke narrates that this behavior generated the opinion that John the Baptist or one of the prophets of old was again at large (9:7-9). Such a way of traveling was a kind of prophetic sign language, not the normal behavior of the needy but the counter-cultural style ("street theater" some might call it) of people with something very new to say. For to travel without a staff left one without a means of defense against unfriendly persons or animals. And traveling without sandals meant one could not run from a threatening situation. It is the traveling style of people taking a dramatically nonviolent posture toward the world. And traveling without money or bread left one utterly dependent upon whatever hospitality might be offered. Moreover, when the rationale is given—"the laborer is worth his wages—" it is clear that this way of doing mission is not an act of indigency but the creation of a new set of reciprocal relationships based on the Kingdom of God heralded in the preaching and demonstrated in the healing. It has been noted that rabbinical rules relating to the temple mount forbade the carrying of a staff, the wearing of sandals, or money carried in a bag or money belt, and that these surprising rules for mission may have meant that "the approach of the Kingdom makes the time a holy season, and the whole land a holy place."[22]

This stark description of the equipment of the immediate disciples of Jesus has led to the theory of a two-tier discipleship: first, the immediate circle of itinerant charismatics who traveled lightly and vulnerably; second, the more settled Christian who owned property but shared generously. That is the picture we get in Luke-Acts. Whether or not they were indigent, both tiers qualified as members of Isaiah's poor Israel, ready to hear and do the word of God.

In Luke-Acts people show themselves to be members of poor Israel by their response to Jesus as God's Prophet, i.e. the one who speaks God's word and does God's acts in their midst. This theme of Israel invited to respond to Jesus as Prophet is further developed in the gospel account and comes to a head in Acts. Those who witness the resuscitation of the son of the widow of Nain glorify God, saying "A great prophet has arisen among us" and "God has visited his people!" (7:16). The disciples on the road to Emmaus, even in their interim darkness, could recognize Jesus as "a prophet mighty in deed and word before God and all the people" (24:19). And in Acts, Peter addresses the assembled pilgrim crowd as "Men of *Israel*," and proceeds to interpret the present events, the Apostles' proclaiming the resurrection of Jesus and challenging the people of Israel to repentance, as something done in the authority of Jesus, now clearly presented by the Father as the "raised up" Prophet-like-Moses. If the people receive the invitation of the Prophet-like-Moses acting through them (Peter and John) they remain members of Israel. If they reject the

---

[22]David L. Mealand, *Poverty and Expectation in the Gospels* (London: SPCK, 1980) 69.

risen prophet, they are cut off from the people. This seems the best reading of the following verses from that speech:

> "Moses said, 'The Lord God will raise up for you a prophet from your brethren as he raised me up. You shall listen to him in whatever he tells you. And it shall be that every soul that does not listen to that prophet shall be destroyed from the people'" (Acts 3:22-23).

Conclusions

Who, then, are the poor to whom the first Lucan beatitude is addressed? The Isaian context (Is 61 in Lk 4:18 and 7:22) points to end-time Israel knowing its need for, and eventually responding to, the salvation of its God. The whole of Luke-Acts further identifies that end-time Israel with those who accept Jesus as God's eschatological prophet to Israel. A corollary theme throughout Luke's double work is that the socially and economically poor turn out to be those most in need of God by virtue of the simple fact that only the needy know they need help. Whence the significance of the presence of the recently sick and demonized, now healed, among the audience of the Sermon of the Plain (6:17-19). In short, "the poor" of the first beatitude are those "true Israelites" who know their need for God. The physically and socially needy have the advantage of experiencing that need most directly. Now we must search for the rich of the woes.

B) THE RICH

1. Old Testament background

First, it should be observed that the contrasting of the poor who trust in God and the rich who trust in themselves has strong OT roots. Psalm 34, especially in its LXX version (the one Luke was likely to have used), is a prime example.

> When the afflicted one [*ptōchos* in the LXX] called out, the
>   Lord heard, . . .
> Taste and see how good the Lord is;

> happy [*makarios* in the LXX] the one who takes refuge
> in him. . .
> The great [LXX: *plousioi*, "rich"] grow poor and hungry;
> but those who seek the Lord want for no good thing [Ps
> 34:7, 9, 11].

Here we have in one place in the Psalms (1) a macarism, (2) a
contrast between the poor and the rich in their relationship
with God, (3) a linking of wealth with hunger and poverty
with satisfaction. The Lucan beatitudes and woes are clearly in
this tradition.

And if we search for examples of the woe-formula in Luke's
favorite prophet, we find that it is indeed Isaiah who uses this
format most frequently, and nowhere more frequently than Is
5:8-23, where the prophet, unfolding the meaning of the parable of the vineyard song, issues no less than six woes against
the arrogant landowners whose property grabbing renders the
countryside desolate, and who are reprimanded for their indul-
gent feasting. They are, in short, addressed as rich, full, laughing and having their consolation now, with only doom to look
forward to.

The subjects of the four Lucan woes (the rich, full, laughing,
and well-spoken-of) are so obviously the opposite numbers of
the subjects of the four Lucan beatitudes (the poor, hungry,
weeping, and reviled) that one is justified in saying simply that
the rich/full/laughing are those who fail to qualify as the
members of end-time Israel because they reject Israel's Anointed One. We must see now whether Luke specifies the identity
and character of the subjects of his woes.

2. Who are called rich in Luke-Acts?

Five *individuals* are called *plousios* in Luke-Acts: three
persons in parables (the rich fool, 12:16; the master of the
crafty servant, 16:1; and Dives, 16:19, 21, 22) and two real
persons, the rich ruler (18:33) and Zacchaeus (19:1). In addition, there are three *generic* references to "the rich": the rich
neighbors Jesus advises his fellow dinner guests not to invite
(14:12); the rich person for whom it is easier to pass through
the eye of a needle than to enter into the kingdom of God
(18:25); and the rich contributing out of their abundance to

the temple treasury, with whom Jesus contrasts the poor widow who "put in all the living that she had" (21:1-3).

However, simply tracking Luke's ten other uses of the word *plousios* does not help us interpret the content of *plousios* in the first woe, for the connotations are mixed. Whereas the parabolic characters of the rich fool and Dives are clearly examples not to be imitated, the master of the crafty servant, the rich neighbors of the table advice, and the temple bene-factors are treated quite neutrally. The rich chief toll collector Zacchaeus, however, turns out to be a good example. And as for the rich ruler, when Luke tells of that man's encounter with Jesus, he leaves the result curiously open-ended. In contrast to Mark and Matthew, who say that the man "went away" after Jesus' invitation to sell all, Luke has him *remain*, as Jesus addresses the eye-of-the-needle saying "looking at him" (18:24-25). Following the *word* for "rich," then, does not give us a precise sense of Luke's notion of what makes the rich of the woes deserving of the prophetic curse. Luke provides this information in another way, in his portrayal of the Pharisees.

3. The Pharisees as stereotypes of the rich

It has become commonplace in NT studies to acknowledge that each of the evangelists pictures the Pharisees in a stereo-typed way. Their portraits of the Pharisees are not so much an attempt at historical record as the presentation of foils who are invested with qualities which are the opposite of those the evangelists wish to highlight in Jesus and the disciples.[23] In Luke, the Pharisees are called "money lovers" (*philargyroi*, 16:14). And there is evidence in other passages of the Third Gospel that Luke portrays the Pharisees as embodying the essence of the "rich" of the woes as contrasted with the "poor" of the beatitudes.[24]

---

[23]I first encountered this insight in G. Baumbach, "Jesus und die Pharisäer," *Bibel und Liturgie* 42 (1968) 112-131, which I later abstracted in English as "Jesus and the Pharisees," *Theology Digest* 17 (1969) 233-240.

[24]For this understanding of the function of the Pharisees in Luke, I am especially indebted to Halvor Moxnes, *The Economy of the Kingdom: Social conflict and Economic Relations in Luke's Gospel*, (Philadelphia: Fortress, 1988) esp. pp. 10-21.

Early on, Luke heightens the presence of the Pharisees as the adversaries of Jesus. In the episode of the healing of the paralytic in Capernaum, they are twice mentioned as Jesus' critical opponents (5:17,21). When the Pharisees challenge the disciples' eating with tax collectors and sinners, Luke alone describes them as murmuring (*egongyzon*, 5:30). They murmur again in another scene of table fellowship with tax collectors and sinners at 15:2 (*diagongyzon* this time). Those words for murmuring ("grumbling," in the NAB OT) describe the resistance against God and Moses in the desert (see esp. Ex 16 and Num 14). The implication is that the Pharisees, and the mentality they represent, lead the way in the resistance of the people to Jesus' leadership in the end-time renewal of the exodus commencing in his ministry.

As in Mark, the Pharisees are the adversaries in the episodes of the sabbath plucking of grain (6:2) and the sabbath healing of the man with the withered hand (6:7). But it is in the narrative about Jesus' words on the Baptist that Luke shows most clearly how he means the Pharisees to be taken as the stereotypical resisters of God's word.

> When they heard this all the people and the tax collectors justified God, having been baptized with the baptism of John; but the Pharisees and the lawyers rejected the purpose of God for themselves, not having been baptized by him (7:29-30).

This description of the Pharisees is immediately substantiated in the episode of the encounter of the woman of the city with Jesus at the dinner in Simon the Pharisee's house (7:36-50). Whereas the Pharisee is unreceptive to Jesus, the woman, though she is called "sinner," expresses her receptivity with the abundant hospitality of her tears and ointment and is said to have the faith that saves (7:50).

The Q source included a stunning excoriation of the Pharisees and scribes. Matthew presents this diatribe as part of the extended encounter between Jesus and the officials in the temple precincts (Mt 23). Luke, on the other hand, presents his version of this material as part of the table talk at still another dinner hosted by a Pharisee (Lk 11:37-52). Regarding the six woes directed here at the Pharisees and lawyers (each introduced by *ouai*, like the woes linked with the Lucan beatitudes), it is the statement introducing them (11:39-41) which interests us, for into it Luke has introduced a concern about money:

> Now you Pharisees cleanse the outside of the cup and of the dish, but inside you are full of extortion and wickedness. You fools! Did not he who made the outside make the inside also? But give for alms those things which are within; and behold, everything is clean for you.

Matthew 23:25-26, apparently conveying the more original Q tradition, has, "Woe to you, scribes and Pharisees, hypocrites! for you cleanse the outside of the cup and of the plate, but inside they are full of extortion and rapacity. You blind Pharisee! First cleanse the inside of the cup and of the plate, that the outside also may be clean." Luke's rendition clarifies the basis of the critique and articulates the remedy. In their preoccupation with external purity laws ("the outside"), the Pharisees have neglected the laws of God regarding just relationships within the community ("those things which are within"). The point of purity laws was to reverence the Creator. But in masking their (internal) greed with (external) manipulation of purity laws, they have offended the One who made both the outside and the inside. The remedy is the conversion from greed to almsgiving. What Matthew merely hinted at, Luke spells out.[25] This is summarized in another way when Jesus says that they "neglect justice and the love of God" (v 42).

The Pharisees intensify their role as adversaries: "As he went away from there, the scribes and the Pharisees began to press him hard, and to provoke him to speak of many things, lying in wait for him, to catch at something he might say" (11:53-54).

At Lk 12:1, the warning about the "leaven of the Pharisees" is called "hypocrisy" and the Lucan context makes it clear that

---

[25]Moxnes explicates this passage in pp. 109-115 of *The Economy of the Kingdom.*

the hypocrisy of the Pharisees is what had just been critiqued in the preceding woes.

In Lk 14, at a dinner to which Jesus was invited by a Pharisee to trap him into healing on the sabbath, Jesus advises his host to try a new kind of hospitality, to invite those who cannot reciprocate, the poor and the unclean (maimed, blind, lame) and thereby open up their closed-circuit hospitality to acknowledge that the ultimate reciprocator is God. Indeed, such a procedure will "beatify" him (he will be *makarios*), because he will be just before God (14:12-14).

In chapter 16, Luke presents Jesus speaking to the disciples on the subject of the right use of money (the parable of The Wily Steward, vv 1-8, interpreted by a poem on Mammon, vv 9-13). This is immediately followed by a description of the response of some other listeners, the Pharisees, and a comment of Jesus (vv 14-15):

> The Pharisees, who were lovers of money [*philargyroi*], heard all this, and they scoffed at [*exemyktērizon*, lit. "turned up their nose at"] him. But he said to them, "You are those who justify yourselves before men, but God knows your hearts; for what is exalted among men is an abomination in the sight of God."

This is a virtual paraphrase of those addressed by the four woes balancing the four Lucan beatitudes:

16:14-15	6:24-26
(*description*)	(*description*)
lovers of money	you that are rich
they scoffed	you that laugh now
you justify youselves before men	all speak well of you
(*consequence*)	(*consequence*)
what is exalted among men is an abomination before God	you shall hunger, mourn, weep

The Pharisees also exemplify a verse in the immediate context which has resonance with the first beatitude:

> And if you have not been faithful in that which is another's [namely, God's], who will give you that which is your own [*hymeteron*]? (16:12)

That is, if you have not been faithful in your stewardship of earthly goods, stewarding what is fact belongs to another, God, how will you receive a recompense that you can call *your own*? Compare, "Blessed are the poor, for yours [*hymetera*] is the kingdom of God (6:20)." It may not be an accident that the rare, emphatic second person plural possessive adjective, *hymeteros*, is used only in these two places in the synoptic gospels. In any case, in the end-time perspective of the beatitudes and woes, the poor have something lasting to call their own; the rich (exemplified especially by the Pharisees) do not.

The three remaining references to the Pharisees, all special to Luke, continue to show to them at odds with Jesus and his cause. When they ask Jesus when the kingdom of God is coming, Jesus tells them it is not coming *meta paratērēseōs*, that is, it is not coming in a way that is perceptible to their way of looking at the world. See 6:7; 14:1 and 20:20, where Luke introduces the verbal form of the noun *paratērēsis, paratēreō*, to describe the manipulative surveillance by which Jesus' enemies try to trap him.

Luke 18:9 introduces the parable of the Pharisee and the Publican with the telling note that Jesus recounts this story to "some who trusted in themselves that they were righteous [*dikaioi*, in right relationship with God] and despised others." Coming as it does on the heels of the parable of the Persistent Widow, exemplifying trust in God, it is clear that the self-righteousness portrayed is, in effect, a denial of God's place in their lives. The parable concludes with the observation that the tax collector went down to his house justified [*dedikaiomenos*, put in right relation with God] rather than the Pharisee. There follows the maxim, "For every one who exalts himself will be humbled, but he who humbles himself will be exalted." The parable well reflects the Lucan beatitudes and woes, with the

Pharisee, as we might expect by now, exemplifying "the rich" and the publican "the poor."

The final intervention of the Pharisees in the Third Gospel occurs at 19:39, where they ask Jesus to rebuke his disciples, who are, on the occasion of Jesus' descending the Mount of Olives on a colt, heralding him as the king who comes in the name of the Lord. They then fade from the picture and have no place in Luke's passion account, perhaps because Luke's passion tradition reflects the historical fact that Pharisees were not influential in matters of concern to the temple authorities.

To summarize, the picture of the Pharisees in Luke illustrates the opposite of what the Lucan beatitudes affirm. They are the very model of what the Lucan woes doom. Their greed has rendered them closed to right relationships with their neighbors and deaf to the word of God addressed to them in Jesus. Thus the Pharisees do indeed turn out to be the opposite numbers of those identified as the poor of the first beatitude.

V. What is Jesus Saying?

Having explored these contextual questions of the identity of the speaker, his audience, the sense of time in history, and the meaning of "rich" and "poor" in Luke, what Jesus is saying in the Lucan beatitudes is becoming clear. The first beatitude sets the tone. It is, first of all, a proclamation about the kingdom. The long-awaited Messiah turns out to be at once the end-time prophet modeled in Is 61 and the Son of God as well. He has been proclaiming to all Israel the good tidings of the Kingdom of God and he has been promulgating it in his healing ministry. The beatitudes and woes are, first of all, statements about what God is doing, ushering in the opportunity for a new set of relationships (human and divine) mediated by Jesus, Anointed Prophet and Son of God.

Since God is offering the gift of end-time salvation through him, Jesus congratulates those in a position to know their need for God's help—the poor, the hungering, the weeping, and those rejected because of their association with him. Because they know their need for God, they are in a position to know salvation when they see it and they will receive it. He can use the ambiguous phrase, "for yours *is* the kingdom of God," because, though the fulfillment is still future, the relationship is already available. It is accessible by association with Jesus, and especially, according to the post-Easter perspective of Luke and his readers, in the life of the Christian community. The poor, hungry, weeping, rejected are congratulated because God has made it possible through Jesus to possess the gift of the kingdom, be satisfied, laugh, and share the lot of the prophets. Conversely, the presence of the Reign of God in their midst in Jesus spells doom for the rich, full, laughing, and well-spoken-of because they are not in a position to accept the proffered gift.

At the same time, if the beatitudes and woes are, first of all, an *announcement* (with attendant congratulations and regrets), they are also an *exhortation*. The mission of Jesus, the twelve, the seventy-two (all foreshadowing the post-Easter mission sketched in Acts), the open-ended images of the elder son in the Prodigal Son parable and the rich ruler staying for the sermon in Luke 18—all point to the further good news that the invitation is still out and the listeners are free to place themselves among either the blessed poor or the cursed rich. This, after all, is the burden of the speech which follows the beatitudes and woes. The listeners are urged (they are free to accept or reject the invitation) to love their enemy, act non-violently and non-possessively, and otherwise to imitate the mercy of the Father. On the level of Luke's readership, even those in the audience who call themselves Christian (i.e., those who called Jesus "Lord, Lord", 6:46) must still decide whether to *do* the word of the Anointed One (and thereby show themselves to be poor like the repentant tax collectors), or *not* to do that word (and thereby show themselves to be rich like the unconverted Pharisees).

The Lucan Sermon on the Plain begins and ends with a set of sharply drawn alternatives. It *begins* with the contrast between the poor, hungry, weeping, rejected on the one side, and the rich, full, laughing, well-spoken-of on the other. Twenty verses later, the speech *ends* with the similitude of the two builders, contrasting those who come, hear, and *do* the words of Jesus (those who build on rock foundation) with those who hear and do not do the words of Jesus (those who build without a foundation). Our analysis suggests that the beatitudes apply to those who are poor enough to be able to hear and do, whereas the woes apply to those who are so rich that they feel no need to hear and do.

The last beatitude deserves our special attention. To refresh our memory, here is the form in which it appears in Luke:

> Blessed are you when men hate you, and when they exclude you and revile you, and cast out your name as evil, on account of the Son of man! Rejoice in that day, and leap for joy, for behold your reward is great in heaven; for so their fathers did to the prophets.

Although some commentators doubt that Jesus said these words, it is not unreasonable that Jesus sought to encourage his closest followers in such a manner near the end of his life. This theme certainly became important to the early post-Easter communities confronted with persecution, as the letter of 1 Peter makes clear (3:14 and 4:13-14). What is also certain is that the community which assembled the sayings of Jesus in the Q document kept the last beatitude with the other three and, by that means, made them explicitly Christian, i.e. linked with the following of Christ. Even more certain is the fact that the evangelist Luke found the last beatitude characteristic of Christian life as he knew it, for he made it thematic to his portrait of church life as sketched in his narrative.

For the Third Evangelist, disciples are prophets who face the probable fate of persecution. Besides the places in Acts where certain disciples are called prophets because they have the special function of prophet within the community (e.g., Acts 13:1; 15:32; 21:10), there are other places where the followers of Jesus are associated with the prophetic tradition in a broader sense. For example, the very imagery which had earlier been assigned to Jesus in the Third Gospel, "a light for the nations," an image from Is 49:6 describing Israel as prophetic Servant of Yahweh, is later applied in Acts to Paul and Barnabas in 13:46-47. That prophetic image from Isaiah is tellingly employed once again at Acts 26:22-23, where Paul, in his defense before Agrippa, speaks of the events of Jesus fulfilling OT prophecies "that the Christ must suffer, and that, by being the first to rise from the dead, he would proclaim light both to the people and the Gentiles." This is a clear identification of the ministry of the disciples as an extension of Jesus' own prophetic ministry. Indeed, their ministry is the very means by which Jesus as risen Prophet-like-Moses now continues his ministry (and fulfills what was spoken of him by Simeon, Lk 2:32).

That sense of the prophetic mission of the disciples is also expressed powerfully in a Q saying found among the woes in Lk 11:47-48. This passage places the Christian prophets and apostles in the line of God's messengers from the foundation of the world through the last book of the Hebrew canon.

Later, at Lk 13:28, where Luke uses the Q saying about the eschatological banquet, which Matthew employs as a commentary on the faith of the centurion, Luke includes "all the prophets" as the first-mentioned guests of the patriarchs:

> There you will weep and gnash your teeth, when you see Abraham and Isaac and Jacob *and all the prophets* in the kingdom of God and you yourselves thrust out.

Three verses later, in response to the Pharisees' warning that Herod wants to kill him, Jesus says that he must continue on his way, "for it cannot be that a prophet should perish away from Jerusalem."

One passage of Acts in particular works as a fulfillment of the last beatitude. After telling of the arrest, flogging, and warning of Peter and John, the narrator continues:

> Then they left the presence of the council, *rejoicing* that they were counted worthy to suffer dishonor for the name. And every day in the temple and at home they did not cease teaching and preaching [*euangelizomenoi*] Jesus as the Christ (Acts 5:41-42).

Besides the covergence with the last beatitude in the elements of rejoicing in being rejected because of the name of Jesus, the use of the word for preaching, *euangelizomai*, is an enhancement of the theme of the apostles extending the prophetic ministry of Jesus, for it is the word Luke took from Is 61. It is used extensively in Acts to describe the mission of the church. It describes the preaching of Philip (8:4, 12, 35), Peter and John (8:25), disciples in general (11:20), Paul alone (13:32; 16:10; 17:18), and Paul and Barnabas (14:7, 15, 21; 15:35).

Hence, for Luke (as for the Q community and, as we shall see later, for Matthew), the last beatitude climaxes the others and makes the following of Christ a matter of following Jesus the rejected Prophet.

VI. Confirmations and Clarifications from Luke's Narrative

Six passages not yet discussed are especially helpful in further understanding Luke's beatitudes and woes: the parable of The Great Banquet, The Rich Fool, the freeing of the bent woman, the parable of Dives and Lazarus, the story of Zacchaeus, and the Magnificat.

A) THE GREAT BANQUET 14:15-24

It should not be lost upon students of the beatitudes that the Lucan version of the parable of The Great Banquet is introduced by two macarisms. The setting is the meal to which the Pharisee (and city council member) has invited Jesus. Jesus has healed a man with dropsy and spoken his parabolic instructions regarding how to be a guest (take the lowest place) and how to be a host (invite the poor, maimed, lame and blind). Jesus' rationale for the latter instruction takes the form of a macarism: "You will be blessed [*makarios esē*, lit. "blessed will you be"] because they cannot repay you. You will be repaid at the resurrection of the just" (14:14). Note that the two clauses parallel the form and content of the beatitudes of the Great Sermon: "Blessed ... you ... for you [followed by mention of divine action]." This statement of Jesus then draws the response of one of the dinner guests in the form of another beatitude: "Blessed is he who shall eat bread in the kingdom of God." The implication is that the dinner has been stimulated by Jesus' reference to divine recompense at the resurrection of the just and now proceeds to elaborate the sentiment by focusing on the image of the end-time banquet.

The parable which follows is not a fresh start in the conversation but precisely a response to the macarism of the dinner guest (v 16 "But he said to him ... "). In this setting, the point of the parable of the Great Banquet is that the table fellowship of the banquet of the kingdom of God is not just a future dream (as the macarism of the dinner-guest implies); it is already a present reality, the invitations are *out* (proffered in the ministry, especially the table fellowship, of Jesus) and people are rejecting the divine invitation in droves. Only the poor and the unclean are accepting the invitation.[26] What we have here, then, in this exchange of macarisms and the attendant parable is the same kind of eschatological tension we found in the beatitudes of the Great Sermon: those poor enough to receive it are in some way already in possession of the kingdom of God; at the same time, the fullness of beatitude and divine recompense remains a future reality.

B) THE RICH FOOL 12:13-21

As in the case of the parable of The Pharisee and the Publican, a statement of the point of the story precedes its telling: "Take heed, and beware of all covetousness; for a person's life does not consist in the abundance of his possessions" (12:14). What follows is an example story which is a veritable cartoon portrait of the subjects of the Lucan woes, a man who is rich, full, laughing (making merry is his aim), and completely out of touch with all the covenant relationships. He has lost his covenantal connection with the land (as the gift of God and meant to be stewarded for the common good), with the community (he communicates only with himself), with himself (the very *psychē* he addresses in v 19 is the *psychē* over which God exercizes proprietary rights), and finally, he has neglected his relationship with God, whose voice intrudes in the end as a complete surprise. Although the concrete danger

---

[26]I am here drawing upon the treatment of this parable in Kenneth E. Bailey, *Through Peasant Eyes: More Lucan Parables* (Grand Rapids, MI: Eerdmans, 1980) 88-113.

of wealth is in view here, the summarizing verse at the end of the story makes it clear that the danger of wealth is what it does to the "bottom line" of one's relationship with God: "So is he who lays up treasure for himself, and is not rich toward God." Like the Lucan caricature of the Pharisees, this rich landowner is a "money lover" (cf. 16:14) who has decided to serve mammon rather than God (12:21; cf. 16:13).[27]

C) THE BENT WOMAN 13:10-17

The healing of the Bent Woman mirrors the Lucan beatitudes in several ways. The very nature of her infirmity embodies the root meaning of both the Hebrew and the Greek words for "the poor" (*ani* and *ptōchos*); both mean "bent over." Her healing is spoken of in language which reflects the jubilary imagery of Is 61 ("you are freed", "*ought* she not to be loosed on the sabbath [the day which commemorates, along with creation, the exodus liberation]?). Her liberation is effected by the word of Jesus. Like the subjects of the beatitudes, she represents those of end-time Israel who are "raised up" because they are poor enough to need divine help (see Acts 15:16, where the same image is used for the restoration of Israel in the Jerusalem community).[28]

D) DIVES AND LAZARUS 16:19-31

This parable reflects the Lucan beatitudes and woes in multiple ways. As in Lk 6, we see the lot of a rich man and that of a poor man contrasted in two situations. One is rich and full, the other is poor and (in words echoing the Prodigal Son, 15:16) desirous of being fed (*chortasthēnai*, cf 6:21; 9:17; 15:16). After death, their situations are reversed. Lazarus now enjoys the end-time banquet with Abraham ("in the bosom of"

---

[27]The exegesis of K. Bailey is most helpful for this parable, too. See *Through Peasant Eyes*, 57-73.

[28]For a fuller development of this interpretation, see my study, "The Freeing of the Bent Woman and the Restoration of Israel: Luke 13.10-17 As Narrative Theology," *JSNT* 31 (1987) 23-44.

is table talk for being in the place of honor next to the host) and Dives is on the outside looking in. Dives is told that he had already received "his good things" in his earthly life and now it is Lazarus who is consoled (*paraklētai*; cf. 6:24, where the rich are told that they have already received their "consolation," *paraklēsis*).

Some commentators understand this parable as portraying a simple reversal: the rich and the poor get their lots switched in a way that has no moral significance.[29] Yet that seems to overlook the implications of vv 29-31, namely, that Dives, like his brothers, had been neglecting Moses and the prophets. If we ask what in the prophets would have been pertinent to the lifetime situation of Dives and Lazarus, Luke has not left us without clues. The larger context from which Luke adds the enrichment of Is 58:6 to Is 61 reads (in Is 58:7): "Is it [i.e., the fast God chooses] not to share your bread with the hungry, and bring the homeless poor into your house; when you see the naked, to cover him, and not to hide yourself from your own flesh?" Dives, distracted by his wealth, has ignored the word of God and suffers the consequences. Nothing is said of Lazarus' piety, except that he experiences what Jews would recognize as the reward of the righteous—end-time dining with Abraham.

What comes as a surprise is that the fates of bliss and doom become effective immediately upon dying. The imagery of Jewish apocalyptic has not prepared the reader for picturing the enjoyment of the end-time banquet immediately after one's death, but that is surely how it is in the cosmos of the parable. Since the imagery of the parable is closely allied with the beatitudes and woes, does this parable indicate that Luke imagines the promise clauses of the beatitudes and woes as fulfilled in divine recompense and judgment after death? The rest of Luke-Acts demands an answer more complex than a simple Yes. We have already heard a macarism from Jesus which points beyond mere life after death to a time of repayment "in the resurrection of the just" (14:14). And we have seen indications of inaugurated fulfillment before death in the experience of the kingdom of God in the ministry of Jesus and the life of the church. Our author is at home with references to the fulfillment of beatitude in three different times: (1) now, in the life of the church continuous with the ministry of Jesus, (2) after individual death, and (3) at the resurrection of the just. In the interpretation of Luke, then, the promises of the beatitudes and woes simply point to the offer of a new future secure before God—a future which can be illustrated by statements about the present life, life after death, or the final judgment associated with the return of the Son of Man.

E) ZACCHAEUS: POOR LITTLE RICH MAN 19:1-10

Into the journey narrative that he has inherited from Mark, Luke has introduced much of his own material. As our author approaches the end of the story of that journey, he begins to bring it to a stunning climax by interpolating the enounter between Zacchaeus and Jesus after the healing of the blind beggar of Jericho. This encounter builds on much that has gone before: the strong woe to the rich (6:24), the devasting parable about a rich fool (12:16), a whole chapter on the foolishness of "moneyloving" (chap. 16 climaxing with the parable of Dives and Lazarus), and the exchange between Jesus and the rich ruler, in which Jesus affirms that it is virtually impossible for a rich person to enter the kingdom of God (18:25-26).

Luke now lays bare the issues by giving us a story which demonstrates the truth of his answer to the question, "Who then can be saved?"—"What is impossible with men is possible with God" (18:26)—the conversion of Zacchaeus. Although this man is rich (he is a *chief* toll collector), he proves open to the offer of salvation present in Jesus. Whereas he is economically rich, in a position to give to the economically poor (see 19:8), he qualifies to take his place among the poor of the first beatitude. As a "sinner" (v 7), and a member of a socially outcast group, tax collectors, he is among the lost that the Son of Man came to seek and save (v 10; cf. 5:29-32 and 15:1-8).

Moreover, it is likely that Luke sees symbolic value in the fact that he is small of stature and exhibits childlike qualities in his desire to see and in his readiness to climb a tree. Indeed, this encounter between Jesus and Zacchaeus exemplifies the saying at the center of the preceding chapter: "Truly, I say to you, whoever does not receive the kingdom of God like a child shall not enter it" (18:17). Zacchaeus received (*hypedexato*, 19:6; cf. *dexetai*, 18:17) Jesus like a child, undergoes a metanoia expressed in his resolve to share his possessions and to make restitution for past injustices, and he hears Jesus utter what is a kind of beatitude: "Today salvation has come to this house, since he also is a son of Abraham" (19:9). At least *this* rich man, having been poor enough to receive the kingdom (as it is present now in Jesus) will be able to enter it in its fulfillment (an issue taken up in the parable of The Pounds, which follows in Lk 19:11-27).[30]

F) MARY: EXEMPLAR OF THE POOR OF THE BEATITUDES 1:45-55; 11:27-28

Within the full context of Luke-Acts, the figure of the mother of Jesus emerges as the clearest exemplar of the poor of the beatitudes. Of the eleven Lucan beatitudes beyond the classic four of the Sermon, three are applied to Mary.[31] Two of them occur in the exchange between a woman and Jesus at 11:27-28, in which the woman praises Mary for her son and in which Jesus says that his mother deserves even greater congratulations for hearing the word of God and doing it- precisely the essential quality of the poor of the first beatitude which our contextual study revealed. The other macarism applied to Mary is the very first beatitude in Luke's gospel, Elizabeth's congratulation: "Blessed is she who believed that there would be a fulfillment of what was spoken to her from the Lord" (1:45).

---

[30]For a recent treatment of the Zacchaeus account as a conversion story, see D. Hamm, "Luke 19:8 Once Again: Does Zacchaeus Defend or Resolve?" (*JBL* 107 (1988) 431-437.

[31]For the record, the fifteen Lucan macarisms are 1:45; 6:20, 2, (two), 22; 7:23; 10:23; 11:27, 28; 12:37, 38, 43; 14:14, 15; 23:29.

Mary's response, the Magnificat, has serveral resonances with the Lucan beatitudes and woes: (1) all generations will call her blessed [*makariousin*] from now on, because of her experiences of God's saving initiative (i.e. she has experienced the Reign of God); (2) the beatitude of the individual (v 48) is related to the blessing of Israel as a whole (vv 54-55); (3) the ultimate fate of the proud, mighty, and rich, is contrasted with that of the poor and hungry. Although Mary is not pictured as indigent, she is poor in the sense of Isaiah and for that reason Luke finds her qualified to sing the song of Israel celebrating the saving action of her redeeming God.[32]

---

[32]For a recent discussion of the origin and meaning of the Magnificat, see Farris, *Hymns*, 108-126.

Part Three

The Beatitudes According to Matthew

Having studied Luke's rendition of the beatitudes, we turn now (with new eyes and ears, it is hoped) to what most people know as the classic expression of the beatitudes, Matthew's eight-plus-one. When I was a child, part of growing up in St. Robert's parish was to commit to memory—along with the Ten Commandments, the Memorare, the Works of Mercy, the Laws of the Church, the Apostles' Creed—the Eight Beatitudes. For good pedagogical reasons, Matthew's beatitudes were "cut and pasted" into the catechism, there to be learned by rote, recited and "saved" in the memory, whence they could be retrieved for prayer and pondering during the years to come. Having on tap such a pool of traditional language is a value perhaps worth recovering today. But there is also a benefit in restoring those classic words to their original setting, the story of Jesus according to Matthew, read against Matthew's own background, especially the Old Testament.

Since Matthew was every bit as creative a theologian as Luke, we shall approach the beatitudes of the First Gospel as we did those of the Third Gospel.[1] Our study of Luke's

---

[1]Quite apart from source theories positing the chronological priority of Mark, the conventional reference to the Gospel of Matthew as the *First* Gospel simply names its traditional place in the sequence of the books of the New Testament canon in printed Bibles.

presentation of the speaker, the audience, and the time has prepared us to follow quickly Matthew's own way of saying much the same thing as Luke. Therefore, we shall cover the questions of speaker, audience, and time briskly in the first section. And, since Matthew appears to be more interested than Luke in developing certain nuances in the variety of images used to describe the blessed and their beatitude, we shall devote more space in the second section to an explication of each of the individual beatitudes.

I. Preliminaries: Who Speaks to Whom, When?

A) THE SPEAKER

Like Luke, Matthew introduces the speaker of the beatitudes as the Son of God addressing end-time Israel. But the manner in which the First Evangelist does this is significantly different. We saw that Luke chose, in his early chapters, to maximize the category of end-time Prophet and to thematize his introduction of Jesus around the titles of Messiah, Son of David, Savior, and Son of Man. Matthew, too, uses the category of Prophet to interpret Jesus, especially, as he approaches the cross, as a prophet much like Jeremiah. But in the chapters leading up to the Sermon, Matthew chooses Christ (Messiah) and Son of God as his preferred titles for introducing Jesus.

It is important, early on, for Matthew to establish Jesus as the one whose very name means that he "will save his people from their sins" (1:21) and as Emmanuel (literally, "with-us-God"). But, for the moment, those names are only seeds planted here for harvesting in the final chapters (see 26:28; 18:20; and 28:20). First, Matthew would use his early chapters to show that Jesus is the Son of God who climaxes, and even *recapitulates in his person*, the history of the people of Israel.

Matthew begins with a genealogy. If Luke's genealogy served to highlight divine sonship in tandem with universal human solidarity, Matthew's genealogy stresses other themes. Matthew first announces Jesus as Christ (Messiah), son of David, and son of Abraham, and then proceeds to elaborate on those titles with the genealogy. This highly stylized recital of the names of Hebrew kings and four foreign women serves several purposes: (1) By punctuating Hebrew history with David (Abraham to David, David to the Captivity, and the Captivity to the Christ/Son of David) and stressing the number 14, the sum of the three Hebrew consonants making up David's name (d+w+d=4+6+4=14), the genealogy highlights the Davidic nature of Jesus' credentials as the Christ. (2) By including the names of highly flawed kings and by the unusual ploy of introducing four women ("outsiders" at that: the Canaanites Tamar and Rahab, the Moabite Ruth, and Bathsheba, wife of a Hittite and possibly from a non-Israelite line herself), Matthew, as Raymond Brown puts it, "is faithful to an insight about a God who is not controlled by human merit but manifests his own unpredictable graciousness."[2] And (3) the genealogy presents Jesus as the culmination of Israelite history. But this son of Israel is also the introduction of something entirely new into its history. Not only is he Son of God in the sense that that title was used for the expected royal Messiah (cf. Ps 2:7), he is also Son of God in a fully transcendent sense, for he was conceived by the Holy Spirit (1:18,20).

Son from *within* history and Son *from beyond*: the narrative continues the dialectic. This Son of Israel begins by reliving his people's story in miniature: threatened with death, he migrates to Egypt and then returns (2:13-23). Matthew underscores the parallel at 2:15 by using Hos 11:1 as a fulfillment citation: "Out of Egypt have I called my son." An image expressing God's special care for *the people* during the Exodus (see Ex 4:22, "Israel is my first-born son") is here applied to Jesus.

Matthew's retelling of the baptism in the Jordan builds a new emphasis into the theme of divine sonship. When we

---

[2] R. Brown, "Matthew's Genealogy of Jesus Christ: A Challenging Advent Homily," *Worship* 60 (1986) 483-490, esp. p. 486. For further reading on the Matthean infancy narrative, the best commentary remains Brown's *The Birth of the Messiah: A Commentary on the Infancy Narratives in Matthew and Luke* (New York: Doubleday, 1977).

compare Matthew's version of the baptism story with the tradition as passed on by Mark, we notice that, in verses 14-15, Matthew has introduced an exchange between the Baptist and Jesus:

> John would have prevented him saying, "I need to be baptized by you, and do you come to me?" But Jesus answered him, "Let it be so now; for thus it is fitting for us to fulfill all righteousness.

"We know that this exchange is not simply an interesting variation in the tradition but more likely the careful expansion of the evangelist, for "righteousness"[*dikaiosynē*] is a special thematic word in this Gospel, used seven times, twice in Matthew's version of the beatitudes. We shall discuss at greater length Matthew's use of this word in our treatment of the fourth and eighth beatitudes. For the moment, suffice it to say that *dikaiosynē* here refers to living out one's relationship with God, or doing the will of God. At a time when the Christian communities were still working out a proper appreciation of the role of John the Baptist vis-à-vis Jesus, Matthew, by way of this little dialogue, is saying, in effect: the question of superior rank is secondary to the more important matter of each person's doing the will of God. At this moment, it was the will of God for John to baptize and for Jesus to be baptized.

Following upon this exchange, the statement of the voice from heaven has a different nuance. Already slightly different in its phrasing—it is now a public proclamation ("*this is* my beloved Son") rather than a private revelation (compare Mark's "*you are* my beloved Son")—the statement now suggests that what makes the Son pleasing to the Father is precisely that he is "fulfilling all righteousness."

This nuance also colors the narrative which follows, the desert testing of Jesus. Whereas Luke's account of the temptations constitutes a commentary on the cluster of baptism-and-genealogy which precedes it, Matthew's version becomes more directly a commentary on the proclamation of the voice from heaven. The three trials are precisely a testing of the Son who would fulfill all righteousness. The fact that Jesus' three answers to the devil come from chapters in Deuteronomy which tell of Israel's disobedience in the desert fits Matthew's literary arrangement well. Already paralleled with Israel as "God's son" (2:15), Jesus now reverses Israel's desert disobedience. Matthew's ordering of the temptations so that the proffered gift of all the kingdoms of the world is now the climactic one, and his placing it "on a very high mountain," evoke the Zion mountain of the Psalm alluded to by the voice from heaven eight verses previously (see Ps 2:6).[3] If, for Luke, Jesus shows himself to be the Son by facing the temptations as a *new Adam* reversing the disobedience of the old Adam, for Matthew, Jesus shows himself as true Son *Israel* (cf. 2:15) by reversing the disobedience of God's son Israel in the desert trials of the exodus experience.[4] The rejection of world sovereignty on Satan's terms here on Matthew's first mountain will finally be vindicated by the granting of world sovereignty on God's terms in the final mountain scene of Mt 28:16-20.

After discovering such a strong use of the category of Prophet in Luke's introduction of Jesus, we may be surprised by Matthew's apparent neglect of that christological tool. In fact, Matthew does not neglect it. Jesus' prophetic role is there in Mt 1-4, but in much lower profile. It exists, first of all, in the discrete parallelism drawn between Jesus and John the Baptist. As in Mark and Luke, John the Baptist enters the scene clearly in the role of the prophet, fulfilling Is 40:3, wearing clothes reminiscent of Elijah, and calling Israel to the wilderness to repent. Unlike the Baptist portrayed in Mark or Luke, however, Matthew's Baptist is a kingdom preacher. Indeed, the Baptist's preaching is summarized in the single line: "Repent, for the kingdom of heaven is at hand" (3:2).

---

[3]Terence L. Donaldson (*Jesus on the Mountain: A Study in Matthean Theology* [JSNTSup 8; Sheffield: JSOT, 1985]) argues persuasively that it is Zion typology rather than Sinai typology which governs Matthew's use of the mountain motif throughout the First Gospel. The primary parallel in the temptations account is not with Moses but with God's son, Israel (p. 99).

[4]See Donaldson, *Jesus on the Mountain*, p. 92: "The heart of the temptations is to be found in an attempt to induce Jesus to be unfaithful to a pattern of Sonship conceived in terms of the relationship between ideal Israel and the divine Father. It is a temptation away from Sonship rather than any specific pattern of Messianism."

Note first that this is an abbreviation and reordering of Mark's introductory summary of Jesus' preaching (Mk 1:15): "The time is fulfilled, and the kingdom of God is at hand; repent, and believe in the gospel." Matthew trims the summary down to its core and, what may be more important, inverts it. He places the imperative first: *Repent*, for the kingdom of heaven is at hand. The call to repent *follows from* the fact that the kingdom of heaven is at hand. Retaining that logical dependency, Matthew phrases the summary so that the focus is now the call to repent. A reading of the remainder of the First Gospel will show that that is indeed Matthew's focus. He presumes that his readers know about the kingdom of God; his concern to urge them to live out the consequences of that blessing. Second, note that the identical summary, used both for John and for Jesus, prepares us to perceive Jesus as picking up the prophetic ministry which was interrupted by the imprisonment of the Baptist (4:12). The parallel between the two is further underscored when Matthew comments on Jesus' debut with a fulfillment citation from Isaiah (Is 9:1-2 at Mt 4:15-16), just as he did for John.

To summarize, when Matthew presents the reader with Jesus speaking the beatitudes, he has introduced him as the Son of God in at least three senses: as conceived by the Holy Spirit, as royal Messiah, and as the embodiment of the people of Israel. Jesus demonstrates that sonship especially in his "righteousness," i.e. doing the will of God. For Jesus in the early chapters of the Gospel, doing God's will consists in extending the prophetic ministry of John the Baptist by calling Israel to repentance on the basis of the present inauguration of the Kingdom of God in Jesus' person and in his teaching, preaching and healing.

B) THE SETTING AND AUDIENCE

Matthew, like Luke, crafts the setting of the Great Sermon very carefully. Like Luke, Matthew's purpose is not simply to pass on what Jesus said on a particular occasion but to capture the essence of Jesus' teaching for those who would be his followers (in Jesus' time and in Matthew's). Further, as in the Gospel of Luke, Matthew provides ample literary cues to signal the framework in which he wishes the words of Jesus to be understood.

The narrative setting.

First, there is the macro-frame established by the nearly identical summaries of 4:23 ("and he went about all Galilee, teaching in their synagogues and preaching the gospel of the kingdom and healing every disease and every infirmity among the people") and 9:35 ("and Jesus went about all the cities and villages, *teaching in their synagogues and preaching the gospel of the kingdom, and healing every disease and every infirmity*").[5] Commentators have noted that this repetition brackets a schematic presentation of Jesus first as Messiah of the *word* (Mt 5-7) and then as Messiah of *deed* (Mt 8-9). This is followed immediately by the mission charge to the Twelve (Matthew omits a separate account of a *call* of the Twelve, paralleling Mk 3:13-19, and moves right to the *sending*, par. Mk 6:6-13), which makes up chapter 10. Immediately after that, the narrator says that John the Baptist heard in prison about "the deeds of the Christ" [*ta erga tou Christou*], a strikingly formal and inclusive phrase which seems to refer to all that has been presented schematically in the preceding seven chapters, the words and deeds of Jesus and the Twelve. Seen within the story line of Matthew, then, the words which introduce the setting of the beatitudes have in view more than the recital of a certain speech; they set the reader up for Matthew's interpretation of the words and deeds of the Messiah and his church.

Didachē and kerygma.

Since the summary of Mt 4:23 (par. 9:35) mentions *teaching* in synagogues and *preaching the gospel of the kingdom*, we might consider the beatitudes (and the accompanying salt/city/light

---

[5]G. Lohfink ("Wem gilt die Begpredigt? Eine redaktionkritische Untersuchung von Mt 4, 23-25 und 7,28f," *TheolQuart* 163 [1983] 277) hears in Mt 4:23 an echo of LXX Dt 7:15, which he finds significant because healing is promised to the full community of Israel.

sayings of 5:13-14) as falling within the category of "preaching the kingdom" (*kerygma*) and the rest of the Sermon as "teaching" (see *didachē* in 7:28 and *didaskōn* in 7:29). For the beatitudes and the salt/city/light sayings are, after all, proclamations, heraldings, and what follows is teaching and exhortation. Further, the beatitudes are a transitional expansion of the summary of Jesus' preaching given at 4:17 ("Repent, for the kingdom of heaven is at hand"): the first member of each beatitude expresses an aspect of the disposition which represents conversion (repenting), and the second member of each beatitude is an expression of the experience of the kingdom either as present reality (5:3,10; "theirs is the kingdom") or future reward (vv 4-9,11-12).

The plenary gathering.

Matthew's description (in v 25) of the origins of the gathered crowd is strikingly broad and inclusive: "And great crowds followed him from Galilee and the Decapolis and Jerusalem and Judea and from beyond the Jordan." This description is more than a way of indicating that people came to Jesus from far and near. The choice of geographical areas reaches beyond the Palestine of Jesus' and Matthew's day to include all four corners of the kingdom of Israel as it existed under David: the Northwest (Galilee), and Northeast (Decapolis, which the Hasmoneans looked to as part of end-time Israel), the Southwest (Jerusalem, Judea), and the Southeast (Perea, "beyond the Jordan")—in other words, *all Israel*, as it was under David and as it was hoped for under the messianic Son of David.[6] In his own way, Matthew is doing what Luke did; he is evoking the picture of end-time Israel gathered around Jesus, a "transparency" of the church.

It is, moreover, not only a plenary gathering but also a *healed* community. *All* the sick of the people of God are brought to Jesus and he heals them. G. Lohfink observes that, just as the deeds of Yahweh preceded the giving of the Law at Sinai so the healing deeds of Jesus precede its end-time ex-

---

[6]Ibid., pp. 274-276.

plication. Before people can obey the radical demands of Jesus, they must be healed.[7] As always in the New Testament understanding of morality, the gift precedes the demand; one is asked to *become* fully what one already *is* as a member of the people of Jesus.

The mountain (among the mountains of Matthew).

Not one but two mountains dominated the topography of first-century imaginations nurtured by the Old Testament, Sinai and Zion. Sinai, of course, was a memory, the place of the giving of the Law, the Torah. Zion, on the other hand, was not only a present reality but also a hope, the place where the Messiah would be established (see Ps 2:6) and where the end-time restoration of Israel and the pilgrimage of the nations would center (see Is 2:2-4; 56:7-8; 60:1-4 and Jer 31:12,23). It has been common for commentators to take Sinai as the symbolic referent of Matthew's mountain. Seen this way, Jesus was acting as New Moses promulgating a New Law. Recently, however, some have argued that the complex of end-time Zion imagery provides the most natural background for Matthew's use of mountains.[8] Is 2:2-4 is one of the classic expressions of that cluster of Zion images:

> It shall come to pass in the latter days
> > that the mountain of the house of the Lord
> shall be established as the highest of the mountains,
> > and many peoples shall come, and say:
> "Come, let us go up to the mountain of the Lord,
> > to the house of the God of Jacob;
> that he may teach us his ways
> > and that we may walk in his paths."
> For out of Zion shall go forth the law
> > and the word of the Lord from Jerusalem.

This end-time vision features a reshaping of the face of the

---

[7]Ibid., p. 277.

[8]See especially Donaldson, *Jesus on the Mountain.*

earth (Zion raised above its surrounding mountains) and the pilgrimage of the nations coming for instruction in the Torah. The verses that follow envision peace ("swords into plowshares," v 4), and light (v 5). Elsewhere the motif of the restoration of Israel dominates, but the cumulative picture that develops, especially during second temple Judaism, is that of Israel restored on Zion in "the age to come," a source of light and peace to the nations who come to join the end-time community.

Matthew's stylized setting and introduction to the Sermon appears to governed by that image cluster, with all the associations usually applied to end-time Zion now ascribed to Jesus. (1) Representatives from all corners of Davidic Israel have been gathered and healed. (2) Gentiles had come to honor Jesus in the infancy narrative. (3) Jesus' public ministry is described in a fulfillment quotation as light introduced into darkness (Mt 4:15-16; Is 9:1-2). (4) The metaphor of "light for the world" applied to the disciples in 5:14 is reinforced with the saying, "A city set on a hill cannot be hid" (the keynote of the Zion motifs). And (5), what follows in the sermon is the end-time exposition of the Torah.[9]

The audience.

As in Luke, the references in the initial chapters of the Gospel to "the people" [*laos*] of Israel prepare the reader to see the scene of Jesus preaching and teaching on the mountain as a matter of Jesus addressing all Israel (see 1:21; 2:1-12; 4:16). We are ready, then, to hear *laos* in 4:23 as meaning all of end-time Israel. Then, as in Luke's setting, the whole becomes stratified when the narrator introduces a distinction between the "great crowds," whom Jesus "saw" (5:1), and the disciples, whom Jesus "taught" (v 2).

Who are these disciples? This is the first time the word is used in this Gospel, and in Matthew's story line, we have learned of only *four* persons who might qualify as disciples:

---

[9]Donaldson (*Jesus on the Mountain*, 118) summarizes this insight well: "The mountain setting of the Sermon is presented by the evangelist against the background of Zion eschatology—though a Zion eschatology interpreted in christological terms: Jesus, and not Jerusalem, is the gathering point for the eschatological people of God and the locus of the renewal of the Torah."

Peter, Andrew, James and John, recently called by Jesus in 4:18-20. Does Matthew have in mind only these four as the primary audience of the Sermon? That would seem odd. When the Twelve are first mentioned in 10:1, they are called "his twelve apostles," as if they had been with Jesus for some time, although up to this point in the story we have seen the *calling* of only six, the two sets of brothers in chapter 4, the one who would bury his father (8:21-22), and the tax collector Matthew (9:9). The evangelist apparently presumes that his readers are acquainted with the tradition of the Twelve disciples. Throughout his Gospel, Matthew appears to confine the name "disciples" to the Twelve, who also serve to symbolize the post-Easter church. The disciples of 5:1, then, are the Twelve, those of Israel who are fully responsive to the preaching and teaching of Jesus, those who qualify as salt and light and constitute the city on the mountaintop.

And the "great crowds" [*ochloi polloi*]? Are they part of the audience, or are they simply a backdrop? The final words of the narrator in chapter 7 leave no doubt that the crowds are part of the audience: "And when Jesus finished these sayings, the *crowds* were astonished at his teaching, for he taught them as one who had authority, and not as their scribes" (7:28-29). The continuation of the story ("when he came down from the mountain, *great crowds followed him*," 8:1) indicates that these words were written with the setting of the Sermon still clearly in mind, for they contain an exact repetition of the first words of 4:25: "And great crowds followed him..."

Jesus' audience, then, is neither all the world, nor scattered individuals, but the community of Israel. Those who respond, who repent and believe in the gospel, become disciples, represented in this Gospel by the Twelve. The rest receive the same invitation. A summary statement of Donaldson is helpful here:

> Just as the Jewish leaders and the disciples function in the First Gospel as transparencies for the Judaism of Matthew's day and for his own church respectively, so the *crowds* represent a segment of Judaism for whose salvation the evangelist still holds out hope.[10]

---

[10]Ibid., p. 208. Guelich (*Sermon*, 59-60) calls the *ochloi* of Matthew "a neutral chorus."

C) THE TIME

It should be clear by now that Matthew is just as concerned as Luke to show that Jesus speaks the beatitudes in a particular time in the history of God's dealing with God's people, the time of eschatological fulfillment. What we have here is the Son of God proclaiming to the people of God the divine end-time intervention that they had been waiting for. The kingdom of God was present in Jesus during his ministry and inaugurated in full strength with his death and resurrection. A second coming and a final judgment by the Son still remain for the future. Meanwhile, the announcement and invitation of the beatitudes is still extended to those of the endtime people who can step forward from the crowds into discipleship, and move from astonishment to faith.

II. The Message of the Matthean Jesus

As we recognized in part one of this book, Matthew's version of the beatitudes is very much *his package*. That is, he has taken the Q version of the sayings and, faithful to the spirit of the originals, he has recast and elaborated them in ways that would better serve his interpretation of that original spirit.

Evidences of literary design are multiple. With respect to their composition, we have two clusters of four with the outer limits (the first and the eighth beatitudes) signalled by the reference to "kingdom of heaven," and the two clusters marked by a reference to "righteousness" in number four and number eight, and the descriptive adjectives of the first four beatitudes joined by an alliteration of *p*-sounds (*ptōchoi tō pneumati, penthountes, praeis, peinōntes*). With respect to redaction, the additions of "poor *in spirit*," "thirsting *for righteousness*," inheriting the land, and the placement of "the mourning" immediately after the beatitude about the poor, all point to an intent on the part of the author to align the beatitutdes even more explicitly with Is 61. These cues help us see that, like Luke, Matthew is working with great care as an author. We must read him, then, as we read Luke, with attention both to the OT background and to the context of the full Gospel narrative.

A) FOR THE POOR IN SPIRIT: THE KINGDOM OF HEAVEN

"Blessed are the poor in spirit, for theirs is the kingdom of heaven." Over the innocent phrase, "in spirit," much ink has been spilled. For some the phrase is an escape ("I can be as wealthy as I want, as long as I am detached"). For others, it is a scandal ("Matthew appears to be 'spiritualizing' the original beatitude about the actually poor"). Still other readers are thrown off by an accident of the English language: by analogy with idoms like, "He is poor in algebra" or "This soil is poor in nitrogen," they hear "poor in spirit" to mean someone who is dispirited or lacking in spirit.

But the phrase is in fact neither a watering down of Lucan "realism" nor a congratulation of the spiritless. First, to deal with the latter distraction, when the Greek language wants to indicate the good of which poor are deprived, it does this by means of the genitive case, not, as here, by the dative.[11] It is then, the same kind of phrase as "pure in heart" (Mt 5:8) and "gentle and lowly in heart" (Mt 11:29), that is, the metaphorical application of what is ordinarily a physical quality to the human interior (sometimes called *spirit*, sometimes *heart*). Most commentators are satisfied to cite the solution of Dupont, who finds a Hebrew parallel to Mt 5:3 in a document from Qumran (1QM 14:7), where *anawei ruach* appears to mean "humble."[12] By another route, however, R.A. Guelich may have come closer to Matthew's intent. Guelich takes his cue from Matthew's alignment of the beatitudes with Is 61 and suggests that it was necessary for the evangelist to add *tō pneumati* if the word *ptōchoi* was to be used in a way that was faithful to its occurrence in Is 61:1. For the word *ptōchoi* at Is 61 is a rare use of that word to translate *anawim*, the more usual word being *praeis* (="meek"). Matthew wants to be sure his language captures the full OT range of *anawim*, which, while retaining the socioeconomic element, puts greater stress on the relationship of the poor to God. "Ultimately, the *poor*

---

[11]Dupont (3:336) makes this observation.

[12]Ibid., p. 461.

in spirit of 5:1, viewed as an explication of Is 61:1, is no
different from Luke's *poor*, since each refers to those who
stand without pretense before God as their only hope."[13]

If this interpretation of Matthew's phrase is correct, it must
also be acknowledged that the socioeconomic dimension of
"the poor" does not carry nearly the thematic weight in
Matthew that it does in Luke. No individual is called *ptōchos*
in the First Gospel, all five instances being "the poor" in the
generic sense (5:3; 11:5; 19:21; 26:9,11). And Matthew has
nothing like the Lucan contrast between rich and poor. Indeed,
only two individuals are called *plousios* ("rich"), the young
man who had many possessions (by implication, at 19:23-24)
and Joseph of Arimathea (also called a "disciple," 27:57; is he
Matthew's Zacchaeus?).

If by "poor in spirit" Matthew intends the same people as
Luke (i.e. those of Israel who know their need for God), what
about Matthew's "kingdom of heaven" (literally, "the kingdom
of *the heavens*," the plural reflecting the Hebrew counterpart,
ha shamaim)? Is it the same as Luke's "Kingdom of God"?

Here again, the English-speaking reader can be distracted
by an accident of the language. For the phrase "the kingdom
of—" is, in English, often used to refer to a place, as in "the
kingdom of England." Since Heaven is the traditional name

---

[13]Guelich, *Sermon*, pp. 74-75. If "the poor" of Luke and "the poor in spirit" of
Matthew are virtually the same use of Isaian language to name *any authentic
Christian*, what are we to make of the contemporary church's "preferential option for
the poor"? Rooted in the Latin American reading of Scripture, confirmed by the
documents of Medellin and Puebla, and appropriated by recent papal statements, this
phrase has become thematic in the thinking of U.S. bishops. In their pastoral letter on
Catholic social teaching and the U.S. economy, *Economic Justice for All*, they urge,

> As followers of Christ, we are challenged to make a fundamental 'option
> for the poor'—to speak for the voiceless, to defend the defenseless, to
> assess life styles, policies, and social institutions in terms of their impact on
> the poor. This 'option for the poor' does not mean pitting one group
> against another, but rather, strengthening the whole community by as-
> sisting those who are most vulnerable (#16)

This option for the poor derives not so much from the beatitude about the poor as
from the more prevalent biblical theme of God's judgment of covenant fidelity by the
criterion of the community's treatment of its neediest members and from Jesus'
concerted choice to minister to the outcast and most vulnerable.

for the place of salvation with God after death, "the kingdom of heaven" can sound like "the kingdom which is Heaven." Understood this way, the first Matthean beatitude could be paraphrased, "Blessed are the poor in spirit, for they shall eventually go to Heaven." But a comparison of the Gospel of Matthew with the rest of the synoptic tradition (Luke, Mark and Q) makes it clear that such is not Matthew's meaning. For Matthew alone among the synoptics uses "kingdom of heaven," and where he parallels Mark and Luke, they always have "kingdom of God." This has led most commentators to assert that Matthew's phrase is a Jewish reverential paraphrase used to avoid the holy name of God.[14] And, clearly, Matthew does mean to say what Mark and Q say by *basileia tou theou*. At the same time, Matthew's word choice cannot be explained simply as a reverential avoidance of the Holy Name, for *ho theos* (the ordinary Greek word for God) occurs at least 47 times in this Gospel, indeed four of those times in the phrase *kingdom of God* (12:28; 19:24; 21:31,43).[15] H. Traub may be right when he suggests that Matthew's use of "heaven" in "kingdom of heaven" is more than a *substitute* for the name of God. It does indeed name God but with a special emphasis on God's transcendence. That is, "kingdom of God" carries the connotation that "God's work, which is sovereign and which brings sovereignty, is an active lordship coming down from heaven."[16] For Matthew's Jesus, God is not simply "my Father" but most frequently "my Father in heaven." "Kingdom of

---

[14]Indeed, the NAB (1970) tries to spare the reader's confusion by frequently rendering Matthew's "kingdom of *heaven*" [*basileia tōn ouranōn*] as "the kingdom (or reign) of *God.*"

[15]Margaret Pamment ("The Kingdom of Heaven According to the First Gospel," *NTS* 27 [1981] 211-232) argues that for Matthew "the kingdom of *heaven*" is an entirely future reality, whereas "the kingdom of *God*" refers to divine sovereignty already accessible in past and present. Her fascinating thesis finally fails, it seems to me, because to support it she must "de-eschatologize" the verses regarding the kingdom of God (6:10; 12:28; 19:24; 21:31; and 21:43) and the parallel statements of 19:23 and 19:24 must be read in two different ways.

[16]H. Traub, "*Ouranos,*" *TDNT* (1967) 5:522. Guelich (*Sermon,* 77-78) also follows this interpretation. The revised NAB (1986) appears to have acknowledged the value of preserving Matthew's nuance by reverting to the more literal rendering, kingdom of heaven.

heaven," then, means kingdom of God, but with the note of sovereignty highlighted.

As in Luke's version of this beatitude, the promise of Matthew's first and eighth beatitudes is expressed in the present tense, "for theirs *is* the kingdom of heaven." In Luke's case, we concluded that the reign of God was understood to have been inaugurated in the person and ministry of Jesus and accessible in the community of the church. Can we say the same of Matthew's first and eighth beatitutdes? When is the kingdom of heaven possessed, according to the Gospel of Matthew? John the Baptist and Jesus announce, and the Twelve are instructed to announce, "The kingdom of heaven has come near [*engiken*, perfect tense]," 3:2; 4:17; 10:7. This speaks of proximity and presence but not possession. "Entering" the kingdom is usually referred to as a future activity (5:20; 7:21; 18:3; 19:23,24; 20:21), although tax collectors and harlots are said to be entering the kingdom of God now (21:31). "Inheriting" the kingdom comes at the final sorting out by the Son of Man (25:34). There is no doubt that Matthew, more than Luke, stresses the second coming of Christ and the moment of judgment attending that event. Coherent with that understanding, we can surely read the promise of the first and eighth beatitudes as reaching its *ultimate* fulfillment at the *end* of the end-time.

However, another series of statements and images from this Gospel suggest that the "possession" is at least inaugurated in current Christian life. "The violent bear it away" (11:12). Jesus' casting out of demons by the Spirit of God is a sign that the kingdom of God "has come upon you" (12:28). The tax collectors and whores enter it (21:31). Those who are like little children own it (19:14). Perhaps most pertinently, two key parables of the kingdom of heaven present an image of at least *finding* the kingdom before gaining total possession: the Hidden Treasure and the Pearl of Great Price (13:44-45). In both cases, the person really does encounter the item that symbolizes the kingdom ("finding is the first act," as Dominic Crossan puts it in the title of a book about the first of these parables). Indeed, the parable of The Hidden Treasure might be considered a cameo of the first beatitude; the man plowing in the field actually *discovers* a hidden treasure and *in his joy* sells all that he has to buy that field; similarly, those who are poor in spirit in the presence of the kingdom of heaven manifest in the Son of God can be called truly *makarioi*, happy, for the kingdom of God is theirs for the taking—that is, for the giving, the "selling of all they have."

B) FOR THE MOURNERS: CONSOLATION

"Blessed are those who mourn, for they shall be comforted."

In our discussion of the Q form of the beatitudes, we observed that one of the arguments for asserting the priority of Matthew's second beatitude over Luke's similar third beatitude ("Blessed are you that weep for you shall laugh") was that Matthew's is a clear reflection of Is 61, already alluded to in the first beatitude. However one settles the question of which is the more original, it is clear that Is 61 provides the context in which Matthew's second beatitude is to be understood. The oracle of salvation immediately preceding this passage had already employed this image (Is 60:20c: "and your days of mourning shall be ended"). Then, in the series of clauses elaborating the prophetic mission outlined in Is 61:1-2, "to comfort all who mourn [LXX: *parakalesai pantas tous penthountas*]" is the climactic function. Indeed comforting the mourning becomes the dominant image of the oracle as verse 3 goes on to elaborate the kind of mourning that is meant: "to grant to those who mourn in Zion—to give them a garland instead of ashes, the oil of gladness instead of mourning, the mantle of praise instead of a faint spirit." If indeed Is 61 is the primary background for understanding it, Matthew's second beatitude is a variation on the first. "Those who mourn" is another description of Israel in need of God's help.

If there is any doubt that the comforting of the mourning is for Isaiah an image of eschatological salvation, some verses of a salvation oracle towards the end of the same prophetic scroll (Is 66:10-11) flesh out the sentiment by means of the metaphor of Jerusalem as a nursing mother:

> Rejoice with Jerusalem, and be glad for her,
> all you who love her;
> rejoice with her in joy,

> all you who mourn [LXX: *pentheite*] over her,
> that you may suck and be satisfied with her consoling
> breasts[*mastou paraklēseōs*].

The passive voice of "for they *shall be comforted*" is the "divine passive," i.e. a semitic circumlocution for referring to an act of God. Unlike the first beatitude, this one states the promise in the future tense. When is that future divine consolation meant to occur? During the time of the church? Or at the final coming of the Son of man? The other place where Matthew employs the word for mourning (*pentheō*) happens to be a passage which shows his editorial hand and, therefore, may provide a clue to the answer.

The case in point is the controversy about fasting (Mt 9:14-17; par. Mk 2:18-22). Asked why his disciples do not fast like those of John the Baptist, Jesus answers, according to Mark's version, "Can the wedding guests fast while the bridegroom is with them? As long as they have the bridegroom with them, they cannot fast. The days will come, when the bridegroom is taken away from them, and then they will fast in that day" (Mk 2:19-20). Matthew has Jesus answer in this way: "Can the wedding guests *mourn* as long as the bridegroom is with them? The days will come when the bridegroom is taken away from them, and then they will fast [*in that day* omitted]" (Mt 9:15).

Several things should be observed regarding the way Matthew's redaction integrates with the rest of the First Gospel: (1) In Matthew's retelling of the tradition, the episode of the question about fasting has become situated in the banquet scene at Matthew the tax collector's place. (2) The whole double episode is dominated by the joy of the age of salvation; the banquet, the images of bridegroom, the new garment, the fresh wineskins for new wine, all underscore the new eschatological moment introduced by the presence of the messianic Son of God. (3) The thrust of Jesus' answer in the setting of his ministry (Stage I) is that the *non*-fasting of him and his disciples (see, too, 11:16-19) is a kind of prophetic action signalling the inauguration of the New Age. (4) The reference to the "days" to come when the bridegroom is taken away and they will fast is best understood as a reference to the post-Easter (Stages II and III) practice of fasting within the church. (5) By introducing *mourn* for Mark's *fast* and by dropping the phrase "in that day," Matthew has highlighted the time reference as a *period* in which the community's practice of fasting is understood as expressing the pain of separation during the interim between Easter and the parousia. (See the parables of The Great Banquet, 22:1-14, and The Wise and Foolish Maidens, 25:1-2, for Matthean images of the return of the Son of man as a bridegroom.) (6) At the same time, fasting for the Christian is not a matter of retrieving "old wine skins," for the sayings on fasting in the Sermon on the Mount (6:16-18) make it clear that Christian fasting is a new creation; in contrast to traditional Atonement fasting, they are to anoint their faces; that is, they are to fast in the manner of people preparing for a feast. Christian "mourning" is a new kind of mourning indeed.[17]

Against this background, Matthew's second beatitude takes on new life. For those who respond appropriately to the gospel of the kingdom of heaven, those who know their need for God's saving intervention in Jesus are "happy mourners," for not only can they anticipate God's final comforting when the kingdom of heaven is fully established; even now in their share in the life of the messianic community, like the finder of the buried treasure selling all he has "in his joy," they perform the "mourning" gesture of fasting in joy.

C) BLESSED ARE THE MEEK, FOR THEY SHALL INHERIT THE LAND/EARTH

The only significant *textual* question that arises regarding the Matthean beatitudes concerns this third one. It has never been suspect as an authentic Matthean beatitude; every manuscript of Matthew has it. What is a matter of debate is this beatitude's *place* in the line-up. Some ancient versions (Jerome's famous Latin Vulgate among them) invert verses 4 and 5, making verse 5 (the poor) come right after verse 3 (the

---

[17]See J. Meier, *Matthew*, 92-96; E. Schweizer, *The Good News According to Matthew*, 227; and especially J. F. Wimmer, *Fasting in the New Testament* (New York: Paulist, 1982) 52-78 and 85-101.

meek). This arrangement results in a nice rhetorical balance:

> Blessed are the poor in spirit,
>> for theirs is the kingdom of *heaven*.
>
> Blessed are the meek,
>> for they shall inherit the *earth*.[18]

However, the vast majority of the manuscripts support the more familiar sequence. And it is easier to suppose that a second-century copiest reversed the order to produce the antithesis than to suppose that a scribe would break up such an antithesis by thrusting the beatitude of the mourners between them.[19] Moreover, the accepted order—poor in spirit, mourning, meek who shall inherit the land—reflects the order in Is 61.

The question of the Old Testament roots of this beatitude is rich. Mt 5:5 is nearly a verbatim quotation of Ps 37:11—"But the meek [Heb. *anawim*] shall possess [the] land, and delight themselves in abundant prosperity." The LXX (Ps 36:11) has "The meek shall inherit land [*hoi praeis klēronomēsousi gēn* ...]." Apart from the lacks of the beatitude format and the definite article before *land*, Matthew's words match the LXX. Psalm 37 is a psalm in the wisdom tradition focusing on the religious problem of social injustice and reflecting on that problem in the light of exodus typology. The righteous, oppressed by the wicked, are urged to trust in God for their vindication. Five times it is said that the wicked will be "cut off" and five times it is said that the righteous/ blameless/meek will "possess land" (the absence of the definite article underscoring the concrete meaning, land as "turf").[20] The psalmist is already drawing upon a long tradition. The exodus conquest

---

[18] The Greek word *gē* (the root of such words as *geology, geography*) can be rendered *land* or *earth*. The Exodus background suggests *land*. But when the context includes *heaven*, the co-ordinate word *earth* seems more appropriate.

[19] B. Metzger, *A Textual Commentary on the Greek New Testament* (New York: UBS, 1971) 12.

[20] My sense of this psalm is especially indebted to the treatment of Luis Alonso-Schoekel, *Trenta Salmi: poesia e preghiera* (Bolognia: Editizione Dehoniane, 1982) 456-464.

of the promised land was spoken of as "inheriting the land" (see Dt 4:1). Conceiving the takeover of Canaan under the image of coming into an inheritance stressed the idea that the possession of the promised land was not so much the result of human conquest as the gift of God.[21] Drawing on that tradition, the psalmist urges belief that God will continue to vindicate the faithful by restoring the landless to their land.

It is fascinating that the Qumran convenanters interpreted this same psalm as referring to end-time vindication. In a *pesher*, or commentary, on Ps 37 found in Cave 4 (4QpPs37[a]), the Qumran community, the congregation of the Poor, is identified with those righteous who shall inherit the land. Inheriting the land in v 22 is interpreted in this way: "The interpretation concerns the congregation of the poor ones; [their]s is the inheritance of all the great [ones;] they will take possession of the high mountain of Isra[el and on his] holy moun]tain they will delight...."[22] This reading of the psalm accords well with the end-time Zion complex established in the setting of the Sermon on the Mount as illuminated by Donaldson.

In the Greek version of the Torah, the word translated "meek" in our beatitude, *praeis* (singular, *prays* [pronounced pra *ees*]) occurs only once—significantly, as a description of Moses in Num 12:3: "And the man Moses was very meek beyond all the men that were upon the earth." Aaron and Miriam had complained against Moses and he does not retaliate but rather lets the Lord vindicate him (his own action is to ask God to heal Miriam from her punitive leprosy). Clearly, Ps 37:11 is in the very same spirit (oppressed? let go, and let God vindicate you).

The other major background piece for the third beatitude in Matthew is Is 60-61. Here, in the immediate neighborhood of the text which provided the first beatitude and second beat-

---

[21]W. Foerster, "*Klēros, ktl.,*" *TDNT* 3 (1965) 758-785.

[22]The translation is from Maurya P. Horgan, *Pesharim: Qumran Interpretations of Biblical Books* (CBQMS 8; Washington: CBA, 1979) 197. I was alerted to the pertinence of the Qumran pesher by I.W. Batdorf, *Interpreting the Beatitudes* (Philadelphia: Westminster, 1966) 80.

itudes (Is 61:1-2), we find the promise of inheriting the land occurring both before and after that text. Is 60:21, immediately following a promise that "days of mourning" shall be ended, reads, "Your people shall all be righteous; they shall possess the land forever [the Greek version: forever they shall *inherit* the land, *klēronomēsousitēn gēn*]." And Is 61:7 goes, "Therefore in your land you shall possess a double portion" [LXX: Thus they shall *inherit* the land a second time]. In LXX Is 61:7, *gē* obviously refers to the land rather than the whole earth. And those who are to inherit the land are the ones called earlier in Is 61 "the poor" [*ptōchoi*]. Interestingly, the Hebrew behind "the meek"[*praeis*] of LXX Ps 36:11 and "the poor" [*ptōchoi*] of LXX Is 61:1 is one and the same term, *anawim*.[23]

Which of these passages, Ps 37:11 or Is 61:7, is the more direct source of our beatitude? I suggest that whatever the source of the wording of the beatitude itself (Jesus, the traditon, or Matthew), a likely process is that Is 61:7 was the immediate inspiration, which, already associated with the *anawim* of Is 61:1, then led easily to the full quotation of Ps 37:11.[24]

All of the above has been suggested by the OT background. The beatitude takes on further enrichment from its context in the Matthean account.

Matthew twice applies to Jesus himself this rare (in the NT) adjective for "gentle, humble, meek"—*prays*. The first instance is in the speech in which Jesus speaks of himself as Sophia (Wisdom) incarnate: [25] "Come to me, all who labor and are

---

[23]This brings home the fact that the first and third beatitudes Matthew are synonymous. Inheriting the land is another way of speaking of possessing the kingdom. Note that, at Mt 25:34, the Son of man as king invites the righteous ones to "*inherit the kingdom,*" which, in v 46, is equated with going into "eternal life."

[24]Regarding the authenticity of the third Matthean beatitude, if we think Jesus was inspired by Is 61:1 to call his followers "the poor" in the spirit of that prophecy, surely he could have been led by Is 60:21 and 61:7 to allude to inheriting the land as well.

[25]Torah-Sophia incarnate, as M. Jack Suggs interprets Matthew's use of the Sophia tradition in his christology (*Wisdom, Christology, and the Law in Matthew's Gospel* [Cambridge, MS: Harvard, 1970]). See also Elizabeth Johnson, "Jesus, the Wisdom of God: A Biblical Basis for a Non-androcentric Christology," *Ephemerides Theologicae Lovanienses* 61 (1985) 261-294 for a thorough review and elaboration of the background of Wisdom personified (Sophia) and the uses of that tradition in New Testament and post-biblical theology.

heavy laden, and I will give you rest. Take my yoke upon you, and learn from me; for I am gentle and humble of heart [*prays eimi kai tapeinos tē kardia*], and you will find rest for your souls. For my yoke is easy, and my burden is light." Notice that this set of wisdom sayings has the feel of the beatitudes: Those who suffer are promised relief in paradoxical terms. Curiously, a yoke spells relief. The yoke is easy and the burden light. Although the "rest" is promised for the future, like the kingdom of heaven, it is already somehow experienced in the shouldering of the yoke. Like the beatitudes, this wisdom hymn captures the mystery of discipleship in which the joy is known in the very cost.

The other instance, Mt 21:5, is equally significant. It occurs in the fulfillment citation combining Is 62:11 and Zech 9:9: "Tell the daughter of Zion, Behold, your king is coming to you, humble [*prays*] and mounted on an ass, and on a colt, the foal of an ass." Obviously, Zerchariah's picture is that of an unexpectedly peaceful king. What is largely overlooked is that the remainder of the prophet's vision (Zech 9:10) includes the paradox of a *dis-arming dominion* over the whole earth:

> I will cut the *chariot* from Ephraim
> and the *war horse* from Jerusalem;
> and the *battle bow* shall be cut off
> and he shall command peace to the nations;
> his dominion shall be from sea to sea,
> and from the River to the ends of the earth.

The fulfillment citation occurs in the middle of Matthew's narrative of Jesus' entry into Jerusalem. In Matthew's redaction of these events, Jesus is thrice hailed "Son of David" and his takeover of Zion is exactly the reverse of the original David's takeover a millennium before. The description of that event in 2 Sam 5:6-12 tells of how the Jebusites mocked the would-be conqueror by saying," You will not come in here, but the blind and lame will ward you off." After David does indeed take over, a saying arises, "The blind and the lame shall not come into the house" (2 Sam 5:8). Precisely reversing this, when Jesus enters the Temple as Son of David, "the blind and the lame came to him in the temple, and he healed them" (Mt

21:14). This Son of David begins to come into his inheritance in a new, non-violent kind of way.[26]

How Jesus as the meek one *par excellence* comes into his possession of the land/earth is spelled out by another set of key episodes in Matthew's narrative, the first and the final mountain scenes. In the climactic temptation in the desert, the devil took Jesus to a very high mountain, showed him "all the kingdoms of the world," and promised to *give them to him*, if Jesus would only fall down and worship him (Mt 4:8-10). Jesus refuses. The Son of God will come into his inheritance only through obedience to the Father (3:15,17). After he demonstrates his sonship on the cross, Jesus can, as risen Lord in the final mountain scene, say, "All authority in heaven and on earth has been given to me." The king has come into his inheritance, not by grasping but by letting go to the Father. The meek one inherits the earth.[27]

Matthew's retelling of the parable of The Wicked Tenants (Mt 21:33-43), recapitulates this reality in still another way. It is, after all, a story about inheritance. Regarding the *son of the householder*, the vinedressers say, "This is the *heir*; come let us kill him and have his inheritance." They kill the son and it is said that the vineyard will be given to "other tenants who will give him the fruits in their seasons" (v 41). Then, after a clear reference to the death and resurrection of Jesus (Ps 118:22 at v 42: the rejected stone has become the foundation stone), verse 43 clarifies this matter of inheritance: "Therefore I tell you, the kingdom of God will be taken away from you and given to a nation producing the fruits of it." The *ethnos* producing the fruits of the kingdom is the church. The kingdom of God continues to be used as a flexible symbol; one can "have" it as

---

[26]While Matthew's literal description of Jesus as *prays* at 11:29 and 21:5 (Zech 9:9) are the passages most pertinent to our discussion, his use of Is 42:1-2 at 12:28 is surely part of the picture. Note, especially, v 22: "He will not break a bruised reed or quench a smoldering wick, till he brings justice to victory."

[27]Walter Brueggemann (*The Land: Place as Gift, Promise, and Challenge in Biblical Faith* [Philadelphia: Fortress, 1977]) offers a stimulating treatment of the whole biblical tradition around the theme of land. On p. 183, for example, he summarizes the OT history of land as gift and grasp. "Kings who grasp lose. Pilgrims who risk are given." Jesus in his death and resurrection brings this dynamic to a climax, to be replicated in the life any disciple.

a faithful tenant now, and one will still "inherit" it as a reward in the future.

Thus, Matthew stands at the end of a trajectory in which "inheriting the land" has evolved from an interpretation of the takeover of Canaan to the end-time promise of the Kingdom of God. At the same time, the image has not become disconnected in some other-worldly sense from its earthy origins. Living out the implications of the Reign of God will have its effects in a renewed stewardship of the land.

D) BLESSED ARE THOSE WHO HUNGER AND THIRST FOR RIGHTEOUSNESS, FOR THEY SHALL BE SATISFIED.

The word here translated as "righteousness"—*dikaiosynē*—has been rendered in a variety of ways in English: "justice" (CCD, echoing the Latin Vulgate), "righteousness" (RSV; NAB, 1986), "uprightness" (Goodspeed), "goodness" (Phillips), "holiness" (NAB, 1970), "to see right prevail [*or* to do what is right]" (NEB), "what is right" (JB), "to do what God requires" (TEV).

Why the variety? In biblical language, the Greek word *dikaiosynē*, and its Hebrew counterpart *sedaqah*, express such a rich concept that no single English word does it justice (no pun intended). "Rightness" catches the root sense of *dikaiosynē*/*sedaqah*, especially rightness of relationship. This language occurs mainly in God-talk in the OT. That is, it is mainly God who is said to be *dikaios* or to have *dikaiosynē* in that God is faithful to covenant relationships with the people of God. A human being is said to be *dikaios* or to have *dikaiosynē* if that person is "right with God," that is, if that person lives out the covenant relationship with God and neighbor. We receive the *dikaiosynē* of God as a *gift*; we pursue our own *dikaiosynē* as a *task*, enabled, to be sure, by the saving *dikaiosynē* of God. Significantly, the primary source for the beatitudes, Is 61, uses "righteousness" both ways: those who receive the end-time blessings of the Lord are called "oaks of righteousness, the planting of the Lord" (Is 61:3c; God's saving gift being the point here) and in verse 8 the oracle of the Lord reads, "For I the Lord love justice [LXX: *dikaiosynē*, as in v 3], I hate robbery and wrong" ("righteousness" here surely referring to right behavior before the Lord).

Although in contemporary American English, "righteousness" is not common in ordinary talk and sometimes carries the connotation of moral arrogance, it is still the best English word to catch the full denotation of the biblical term.[28]

We concluded earlier that Luke's short version of this beatitude most likely reflects the Q version. We have good reason to take the phrase, "and thirst for righteousness" as the addition of Matthew, for, apart from the word's occurrence in Lk 1:75 (in the Benedictus), Matthew is the only evangelist to use *dikaiosynē*. Given the rich biblical possibilities of *diakiosynē*, what is Matthew's meaning for that word in this beatitude? Is the righteousness meant here the divine gift or the human task? The other six Matthean uses of the word are instructive:

Mt 5:20. "For I tell you, unless your *dikaiosynē* exceeds that of the scribes and the Pharisees, you will never enter the kingdom of heaven." The parallel "entrance saying" at Mt 7:21 helps us understand what "righteousness" means here: "Not every one who says to me, 'Lord, Lord,' shall enter the kingdom of heaven, but he who does the will of my Father who is in heaven." What follows 5:20 confirms that "doing the will of God" is indeed what is meant by *dikaiosynē* here, for verse 20 introduces the six antitheses (5:21-48). The antitheses call disciples to *do* the will of God in the deeper way of Jesus.

Mt 6:1. "Beware of practicing your *dikaiosynē* before men in order to be seen by them...." Here *dikaiosynē* refers to the practices of piety discussed in the seventeen verses which follow: almsgiving, prayer, and fasting. Here *dikaiosynē* signifies doing the will of God as expressed in those practices.[29]

This sense of "righteousness" fits well the two uses of that word which occur with regard to John the Baptist.

---

[28]Helpfully, the 1986 revision of the NAB translation of the NT renders Matthew's sevenfold use of *dikaiosynē* "righteousness" in each instance.

[29]Helpful literature on *dikaiosynē* in Matthew: J. Dupont, *Béatitudes* 3:209-384; Guelich, *Sermon*, 83-88; J. Lambrecht, S.J., *Sermon*, 107-117; J. Reumann [with responses by J. A. Fitzmyer, S.J., and J. D. Quinn], *"Righteousness" in the New Testament* (New York: Paulist, 1982); G. Schrenk, *"Dikē, ktl.,"* TDNT 2 (1964) 174-225.

Mt 3:15. When John the Baptist protests that *he* should be baptized by *Jesus*, Jesus says, "Let it be for now; for thus it is fitting to fulfill all righteousness." We saw in our earlier discussion of this passage that fulfilling all righteousness here means doing God's will.[30]

Mt 21:32. After the clearing of the temple, when the chief priests and the elders of the people question Jesus regarding the source of his authority, Jesus confronts them with their hypocrisy: "Truly, I say to you, the tax collectors and the harlots go into the kingdom of God before you. For John came to you in the way of *dikaiosynē*, and you did not believe him, but the tax collectors and the harlots believed him," The immediate context, the parable of The Two Sons (21:28-31) with its point of active obedience, indicates that "righteousness" here refers to repentance expressed in action.

The four uses of *dikaiosynē* discussed so far stress the *demand*, or *task*, aspect of the biblical notion of righteousness. But now we must examine the *dikaiosynē* saying in the Sermon on the Mount that has the most in common with the fourth beatitude and that seems to point to another dimension of the righteousness theme.

Mt 6:33. This verse is best understood in the light of the two preceding verses:

> Therefore do not be anxious, saying, 'What shall we eat?' or 'What shall we drink?' or 'What shall we wear?' For the Gentiles seek all these things; and your heavenly Father knows that you need them all. But seek first his kingdom and his *dikaiosynē*, and all these things shall be yours as well [literally, "shall be added on to you"].

Note here that "seeking the *dikaiosynē* of God" is contrasted with seeking food and drink, hungering and thirsting, the very stuff of the metaphor in the fourth beatitude. In 6:33, what is sought (hungered and thirsted for) is not an action to be done but a gift to be given by God. As a commentary on the Our Father, this portion of the Sermon is saying, in effect, Focus

[30]See p. 71.

first on "Thy kingdom come" and the gift and task of "our daily bread" will be added on.[31]

Mt 5:6. In the light of our discussion of five of Matthew's seven *dikaiosynē* passages, the fourth beatitude most resembles the saying of 6:33. That is, those blessed are those who seek first the gift of a right relationship with God. Their hunger and thirst shall be satisfied.[32] As Guelich puts it, "With the extended subject of 5:6, the evangelist summarizes the first four Beatitudes by describing the poor, mourning, meek, and hungry and thirsty as those who, conscious of their own inabilities and dependency upon God alone, turn to him for his acceptance and help."[33]

Having surveyed the other six uses of *dikaiosynē* in this order, we are in a good position to appreciate the dimension of "righteousness" present in the seventh use, the eighth beatitude:

Mt 5:10. "Blessed are those who are persecuted for *dikaiosynē*'s sake, for theirs is the kingdom of heaven." Since persecution obviously follows upon action, carrying out the mission of the church (see 5:11; 10:23 and 23:34), "righteousness" here clearly refers to the active meaning of doing the will of God that we saw in 3:15; 5:6; 5:20; 6:1 and 21:32.

Looking at the two uses of *dikaiosynē* in the beatitudes, then, we can say that "righteousness" in the fourth beatitude stresses the gift aspect and in the eighth it stresses the demand. The shift in emphasis reflects the very design of Matthew's

---

[31]Regarding this verse, Reumann (*"Righteousness"*, 131) notes, "God's righteousness is an eschatological gift but it demands a fruitful response." Fitzmyer (*"Righteousness"*, 219) observes, "One does not seek one's own righteousness but God's." For the opinion that *dikaiosynē*, even in 6:33 means doing the will of God, see Dupont (3:303) and Lambrecht (*Sermon*, 109-110).

[32]Thus Schrenk (198), Reumann (128), Fitzmyer (218). The word for being satisfied, *chortazō*, occurs three times elsewhere in Matthew, all in the two feeding accounts, at 14:20 and 15:33,37, where "the lost sheep of the house of Israel" simply follow Jesus, come for healing (15:29-31), and receive the fruits of his compassion. Regarding the second healing, Donaldson (*Jesus on the Mountain*, 135) makes a good case that the feeding of the four thousand is for Matthew an occurrence on Jewish soil (in contrast to Mark's version).

[33]Guelich, *Sermon*, 102-3.

redaction of the beatitudes, with the first four focusing on attitudes and the second four on actions.[34]

E) BLESSED ARE THE MERCIFUL, FOR THEY SHALL OBTAIN MERCY.

The subjects of this beatitude are described by an adjective rare in the NT, *eleēmōn*. It occurs only here and in the letter to the Hebrews (Heb 2:17), where it describes Jesus ("a merciful and faithful high priest in the service of God"). Dupont notes that, in the LXX, the adjective occurs mainly as a quality of God (25 out of 30 times). The same is true of the noun and verb forms of the mercy word group. The noun, *eleēos*, is a quality of God 236 times and of human beings 60 times. The verb, *eleēō*, 100 times describes an action of God and describes a human action 30 times. A similar divine/human ratio obtains in the NT, with *eleēos* occurring as a quality of God 20 times, and as a human quality 7 times; and *eleēō* describes a divine action 15 times, and a human action three times.[35]

This biblical concept of (mainly divine) mercy has two main meanings, *pardon* granted to the guilty (e.g. Ex 34:6-7) and *help* for those in need (Ex 22:27).

In what sense do the subjects of the fifth Matthean beatitude have this God-like quality? The evidence points to forgiveness as the primary meaning here. For the Q version of the Sermon

---

[34]Is the "righteousness" of the fourth and eighth Matthean beatitudes (sometimes translated "holiness" or "justice") related in any way to social justice as that phrase has come to be used in Roman Catholic teaching? First, *dikaiosynē* and *justitia* are not simply equivalents. *Dikaiosynē*, on the human side, is the rightness that comes from doing the will of God, the faithful living out of one's covenant relationships, human and divine. *Justitia*, one the other hand, is the virtue of giving other persons what is theirs, *suum cuique*—whether "the other" is persons considered individually (commutative justice), or collectively (social justice), or individuals as governed by the state (distributive justice). Although it is possible to describe justice relationships without explicit reference to God, that is not the case with biblical *dikaiosynē*. Thus, while the *dikaiosynē* ("righteousness") of the Matthean beatitudes is not simply equated with social justice, it is fair to say that the Roman Catholic tradition of justice, social and otherwise, is a spelling out of the implications of the larger idea of biblical *dikaiosynē*. The gift and task of biblical righteousness necessarily demands working for social justice.

[35]Dupont, *Béatitudes* 3:604.

material contains the saying: "Be merciful even as your Father is merciful" (Lk 6:36).[36] Matthew's parallel to that verse in the body of his Sermon on the Mount is "You, therefore, must be *perfect* [*teleioi*], as your heavenly Father is perfect [*teleios*]" (Mt 5:48).

Because Matthew introduces the same rare word *teleios* into his version of the synoptic story of the rich young man (19:21 "If you would be *perfect*"; cf. Mk 10:21: "You lack one thing"), most exegetes think Lk 6:36 is the more original version of the Q saying. If that Q saying is Matthew's source, then forgiveness is the main meaning, for the saying in the Q context (as reflected in Lk 6:36) marks a transition from the command to love enemies (Lk 6:32-35) to the exhortation to refrain from judging so as to avoid being judged precisely the pattern of the beatitude. In Matthew's Sermon, these sayings about refraining from judgment are presented at Mt 7:1-2, but they are stated in words even more like the beatitude in Matthew's elaboration of the final petition of the Our Father (6:14-15): "For if you forgive men their trespasses, your heavenly Father also will forgive you; but if you do not forgive men their trespasses, neither will your Father forgive your trespasses."

The best Matthean commentary on the fifth beatitude, however, is the parable of The Unforgiving Servant (18:23-35). In this story a servant is forgiven an impossible, indeed a virtually unthinkable debt—ten thousand talents. (Figure a talent = 6000 days' wages of a laborer; 10,000 talents would mean 60 million days'—or over 164,000 years'—wages!) This servant shortly happens upon a fellow servant who owes him a hundred denarii (that means a mere hundred days' wages) and he has him put in a debtors' prison. Hearing of this, his master confronts the unforgiving servant with the obvious (vv 32-33) : "You wicked servant! I forgave you all that debt because you besought me; and should not you have had mercy [*eleēsai*] on your fellow servant, as I had mercy on [*eleēsa*] you?" This story, remember, was introduced as an elaboration of reponse

---

[36]The Greek word for "merciful" here is *oiktirmōn*, a synonym often found in tandem with *eleēmōn* in the LXX (e.g. Ex 34:6; Pss 85:15; 102:8; 144:8) in a stereotyped phrase usually translated "compassionate and merciful."

to Peter's question, "Lord, how often shall my brother sin against me, and I forgive him? As many as seven times?" And Jesus said to him, "I do not say to you seven times, but seventy times seven" (vv 21-22).

This parable provides a necessary framework for catching Matthew's understanding of the beatitude of the merciful. As in the promises of being comforted and being satisfied, the promise translated "they shall obtain mercy" is a passive verb in the Greek, *eleēthēsontai*. Since "they shall be had mercy on" would be abominable English, the word is rendered in the active construction, "shall obtain mercy." But it is really another divine passive, referring to a future act of God. It clearly points to final eschatological fulfillment. But are we to understand the beatitude to say simply that those who forgive now will be forgiven by God in the end? The parable of the unforgiving servant reminds us that there is more to the good news than that. As finding is the first act in the parable of the hidden treasure, being forgiven is the first act here. The servant's obligation to forgive derives from the amazing largess of forgiveness he had first received from his master. It is that way for those congratulated in the fifth beatitude as well.

Healed, and in the presence of the Messiah who ushers in the beginning of the end-times, Christian disciples know the unexpected forgiveness of the king. They are enabled to be *eleēmones* because they had first experienced the forgiveness of God as mediated by Jesus' healing and forgiving ministry. (Matthew heightens this dimension of Jesus' mediating divine mercy by having clients address him with some variation of *kyrie eleēson* at key moments: see 9:27 [blind men]; 15:22 [Canaanite woman]; 17:15 [father of the epileptic boy]; 20:30-31 [blind men]).[37] While a final fulness of God's mercy awaits

---

[37]This dimension of mercy as help for the needy is expressed redactionally by Matthew in other ways as well. Twice, he introduces into Jesus' defense of his fracture of minor laws of Torah piety a quotation from Hosea 6:6, "I desire mercy, and not sacrifice": at 9:13 (defending table fellowship with tax collectors and sinners) and 12:7 (defending the disciples' right to pluck grain on the sabbath to satisfy their hunger, cf. 12:1). The comment of O. L Cope (*Matthew: A Scribe Trained for the Kingdom of Heaven* [CBQMS 5; Washington: Catholic Biblical Association of America, 1976] 68) is helpful regarding the interpolation of Hos 6:6: "Thus he interprets *sacrifice* not as cultic ritual but as literalistic observance of the *minor* rules of the oral and written

the faithful, the experience of that mercy, like the presence of the kingdom of heaven, has already been inaugurated through Jesus.[38]

F) BLESSED ARE THE PURE IN HEART, FOR THEY SHALL SEE GOD

I would guess that most Christian readers spontaneously associate this beatitude with sexual morality. Specifically, they understand the pure in heart to be those who steer clear of "impure thoughts." There is good reason for this spontaneous link, for the next mention of *heart* in this Gospel occurs twenty verses later on the Sermon, "But I say to you that every one who looks at a woman lustfully has already committed adultery with her in his heart" (5:28). To be sure, this is part of what the sixth beatitude means, but the Old Testament background and the rest of the Gospel of Matthew indicate that purity of heart is a much fuller symbol.

The most obvious background for this beatitude is Ps 24:3-6:

> Who shall ascend the hill of the Lord?
>   And who shall stand in his holy place?
> He who has clean hands and a pure heart,
>   who does not lift up his soul to what is false,
>   and does not swear deceitfully.
> He will receive blessing from the Lord,
>   and vindication from the God of his salvation.
> Such is the generation of those who seek him,
>   who seek the face of the God of Jacob.

Torah. Through Hos 6:6 Matthew establishes the principle that where Torah-piety and the interets of mercy conflict, mercy should prevail." Further, in the fourth woe in Matthew 23:23, the evangelist appears to edit the Q form of the saying (cf. Lk 11:42) by replacing "love of God" with "mercy and faith." Finally, the seven works performed by the righteous (or neglected by the unrighteous) in Mt 25:31-46 are conventionally named the works of mercy in rabbinical tradition (Dupont, *Béatitudes*, 3:627). Thus, mercy as meeting the neighbors' needs is also within the scope of the fifth beatitude.

[38]Guelich (*Sermon*, 104-105) treats this dimension cogently.

What connects the beatitude with this psalm is the linking of *purity of heart* with the prospect of access to the *face of God* (which is conventional biblical language for *seeing God*).[39] This is an entrance psalm, composed in the voice of a pilgrim about to enter the Jerusalem temple. The language about cleanness and purity, then, is to be understood in the cultic or ritual sense. But notice that the psalm participates in the prophetic tradition which interiorizes cultic language. That is, it takes talk about "clean and unclean," which was traditionally used to designate spaces, times, persons and things which were set aside and dedicated to God in a special way (the pure, or kosher), and it applies that language to the whole of the pilgrim's person and life.

The person fit to "ascend the hill of the Lord" (enter the temple to worship) is one whose whole life—in external action, as represented by the hands, and internally, as represented by the *heart*—is dedicated to God (thus called "clean").[40] The pure-hearted pilgrim of this psalm, then, is a person whose whole being is fit for divine worship because the dedication is total. Indeed, the initial verse of the psalm appears to wipe out the notion of clean and unclean in creation, for it declares that all is God's: "The earth is the Lord's and the fulness thereof, the world and those who dwell therein; for he has founded it upon the seas, and established it upon the rivers." The pure-hearted person is the one who has recognized this and lived as creature among fellow creatures.

This contrast between ritual purity and the superior purity of heart manifested in just and merciful behavior is a strong theme in the sayings of Jesus and a special interest for Matthew. That contrast is evident in the addition of Hos 6:6 (mercy, not sacrifice) at 9:13 and 12:7 (as discussed in connection with the previous beatitude on the merciful). In his treatment of the parable of the Sower and its interpretation, Matthew highlights *heart*-talk: he extends the reference to Is 6

---

[39]See M. L. Barré, "Blessed are the Pure of Heart," *Bible Today* 22 (1984) 236-242.

[40]The social side of this dedication is strengthened in the Greek version of verse 4, which goes, "who has not lifted up his soul to vanity, nor sworn deceitfully *to his neighbor.*"

at 13:15 to include, "For this people's *heart* has grown dull . . . lest they should understand with their *heart*," and he then goes on to add those words to the interpretation which follows, so that bringing forth a fruitful harvest becomes a matter of receiving the word in the *heart* and *understanding* it (13:19,23). Again, in the treatment of Jesus' words on what truly renders a person "unclean," Matthew heightens the connection between heart and external behavior by emphasizing *actions* in his list of what proceeds from the heart: (after evil thoughts) murder, adultery, fornication, theft, false witness, slander (cf. Mark's inclusion of coveting, envy, pride in Mk 7:21-22). Again, in the parable of the unforgiving servant, the climax reads, "So also my heavenly Father will do to every one of you, if you do not forgive your brother *from your heart* (literally, "if each of you does not forgive his brother from your hearts [*apo tōn kardiōn*]," indicating a whole community called to forgiveness from the heart).

Perhaps most important of all, the whole thrust of the six "antitheses" of the Sermon on the Mount (5:21-48) is to move disciples from preoccupation with external actions to the interior source of those actions. The focus is on the heart, where one can nurse anger, foster lust, distinguish between breakable and unbreakable oaths, calculate a balance of vengeance, and withhold love from the enemy. And yet the summons is to *action* rooted in a properly dedicated heart: actions of reconciliation, removing obstacles, saying a simple "Yes" or "No", turning the cheek, giving over the cloak, going the extra mile, and letting one's love expand to be as inclusive as the Father's sun and rain.

Both the OT background and the Matthean background, then, clarify the meaning of this sixth beatitude. To a gathered and healed end-time Israel, the Messiah congratulates those who respond to God's fresh initiative in his ministry by letting their whole lives and persons become dedicated (cleansed, set aside) to God. Already enjoying the presence of the risen Son, they shall, in the end, know the divine presence face to face.

G) BLESSED ARE THE PEACEMAKERS, FOR THEY SHALL BE CALLED "SONS" OF GOD

This beatitude presents two stumbling blocks for many contemporary readers. First, when we read "peacemaker," we tend to project onto that word what we usually mean in our contemporary language, and thereby neglect to question what peacemaking might mean for Matthew. Second, when we hear "sons of God," many of us reach for more inclusive language like "children of God," and thereby miss the connection with the other references to son(s) of God surrounding this beatitude.

As for the first stumbling block, we have some warrant for projecting our contemporary ideas onto "peacemakers," for the word itself appears to have come into the English language by way of this beatitude. The *Oxford English Dictionary* cites, as the first (1436) written use of "peacemakers," a poetic reference to Mt 5:9. And the 1534 Tyndale version of Mt 5:9 reads "Blessed are the peacemakers." But, while our modern English word "peacemakers" may have come from this beatitude, we must still try to discipline ourselves to hear *eirēnopoioi* against our best reconstruction of Matthew's background.

Although the OT has no noun (or adjective) we would translate "peacemaker,"[41] the Hebrew word for peace, *shalom* (and its usual Greek counterpart in the LXX, *eirēnē*) means not simply absence of war but much more: the fullness of life, abundance, right relationships all round. *Shalom* is mainly a gift of God, and if there is a peace maker in the OT, it is God. The most immediate background for our beatitude is the rabbinical *asah shalom*, which refers to the establishment of peace and concord between human beings.[42]

If we have been right in identifying, with Donaldson, the Matthean mountain of the beatitudes with endtime Zion, then we should note that the prime Zion text of Is 2:1-4 contains

---

[41] But see Prov 10:10 LXX for the one occurrence of the verb *eirenopoieō*: "He who winks at a fault causes trouble but he who frankly reproves promotes peace."

[42] See W. Foerster, "*Eirene ktl.*," *TDNT* 2 (1964) 419.

one of the most powerful images in the OT regarding peace-making:

> and they shall beat their swords into plowshares, and their
> spears into pruning hooks; and nation shall not lift up
> sword against nation, neither shall they learn war any more.

If the Zion mount of Is 2 was in Matthew's focus, then that accompanying image was surely in his purview. It is important to recognize that this state of affairs is describing an act of God: "He shall judge between the nations and shall decide for many peoples ... "

Perhaps the most important clue to Matthew's understanding of this beatitude lies in the other stumbling block, the promise, "they shall be called sons of God." Our contemporary sensitivity to the apparently non-inclusive nature of the phrase *sons of God* catches our attention. The more inclusive, generic word, *tekna* ("children") was available to Matthew (indeed, it occurs fifteen times in this gospel).[43] But the author chooses here to use "sons of God." The reason may well be that the phrase ties in with the title Son of God used so powerfully for Jesus in the early chapters of this gospel. Recall how the title Son occurred at 2:15 ("Out of Egypt have I called my son"—Hos 11:1), 3:17 (the divine affirmation at the baptism), and the trials in the desert (4:3,6). Above all, "Son of God" in these episodes connotes Jesus' obedience to the Father. The natural association carried by the promise of the seventh beatitude, then, is that the peacemakers somehow participate in Jesus' obedient sonship, and become part of the new Israel that he heads up (2:15). What kind of behavior Matthew has in mind becomes clear as the Sermon progresses and we read the sixth antithesis:

> You have heard that it was said, 'You shall love your
> neighbor and hate your enemy.' But I say to you, Love your
> enemies and pray for those who persecute you, *so that you
> may be sons of your Father who is in heaven;* for he makes

---

[43]The phrase "children of God" *[tekna tou theou]*, however, turns up only in Pauline and Johannine writings (see Jn 1:12; 11:52; Rom 8:16,21; Phil 2:15; 1 Jn 3:1,2,10; 5:2).

his sun rise on the evil and on the good, and sends rain on the just and on the unjust. For if you love those who love you, what reward have you? Do not even the tax collectors do the same? And if you salute only your brethren, what more are you doing than others? Do not even the Gentiles do the same? You, therefore, must be perfect, as your heavenly Father is perfect. (Mt 5:43-48)

Ironically, what first appeared to be a non-inclusive title (because of its sexist ring in our contemporary ears), namely "sons of God," becomes a vehicle of Jesus' most radical call to *inclusive* love. We, men and women alike, are to become "sons of the Father" in our imitation of the Creator's universal benevolence, the kind of inclusive love symbolized in our nurturing God's prodigally showered gifts of sunshine and rain upon *all.*

There are also two places in Matthew's narrative material where he appears to take special care to present Jesus as quite the opposite of the warrior: (1) his application of the First Servant Song (Is 42:1-4) to Jesus and (2) his narrative of the entry into Jerusalem.[44]

The Servant Son (Is 42 in Mt 12:13-21)

Does Mt 12:13-21 portray Jesus as a peacemaker? After the episode about healing the man with the withered hand on the sabbath, Matthew follows Mark by including a summary reference to Jesus' healing ministry. As in Mark's narrative, this has the effect of setting up a sharp contrast between the Pharisees' violent intentions (see v 14: "But the Pharisees went out and took counsel against him, how to destroy him"). Matthew proceeds to heighten that contrast (1) by explicitly interpreting Jesus' withdrawal as a *response* to the Pharisees' murderous plot ("Jesus, aware of this, withdrew") and (2) by including here his longest fulfillment citation, a loose quotation

---

[44]In this regard, Mt 26:52-53, Jesus' word to the disciple who would use swordplay in his defense should not be overlooked: "Put your sword back into its place; for all who take the sword will perish by the sword. Do you think that I cannot appeal to my Father, and he will at once send me more than twelve legions of angels?"

of Is 42:1-4, which describes the mission of the *pais* (meaning either "servant" or "son") "who will not break a bruised reed or quench a smoldering wick, till he brings justice to victory; and in his name will the *Gentiles* hope." This is a picture of a messianic mission of *shalom*, healing and justice accomplished with special gentleness regarding the weak. It is a mission of peacemaking which looks toward (12:14) and beyond the cross to the fulfillment of the final commission, making disciples of all the nations, baptizing them *in the name* of the Father and of the Son and of the Holy Spirit.[45]

The "triumphal" entry

As we observed earlier, in our discussion of the title Son of David, Matthew's rendition of Jesus' entry into Jerusalem highlights the contrast between the peaceful kingship of the Son of David and the warlike kingship of the original David.[46] This contrast between the peacemaking son of David and the warrior David is confirmed when Jesus enters the temple and heals the blind and the lame (unlike David who, upon his capture of the capital, ordered that the blind and lame be slain; see 2 Sam 5:8).

Jesus' way of making peace will, of course, place him where he must suffer violence from others. Only after the crucifixion and the resurrection will the Lord be able to exercise "dominion from sea to sea (Zech 9:10)." The Risen Jesus makes this claim in his final appearance as he commissions the eleven to the peacemaking task of discipling all nations (28:16-20).[47]

Those who are congratulated in the seventh beatitude, then, are not simply the peaceful and the reconciling. They are those

---

[45]Commentators (e.g., Schweizer, *Matthew* 282; Meier, *Matthew* 132) note that the version of Is 42 which Matthew uses is reminiscent of the baptism scene, especially if *pais* is understood as *son*. Two other elements reinforce this connection: (1) the mention of God's Spirit and (2) the use of the verb *eudokeō* ("to be well pleased"). Not only does *eudokeō* occur in the baptism; Matthew introduces it into that other parallel to the baptism scene, the transfiguration: "This is my beloved Son, *with whom I am well pleased* [*en hō eudokēsa*; lacking in Mk 9:7]; listen to him" (17:5).

[46]See p. 90.

[47]Matthew makes a subtle preparation for linking Jesus' peaceful kingship with his death and resurrection by his use of apocalyptic "earthquake" imagery. The description of the response of the city in 21:10 makes it figuratively a "seismic" disturbance—"all

who so participate in the Father's peacemaking initiative in Jesus that they are called by God to share, male and female alike, in Jesus' sonship. Given rootedness in that sonship, our multiple efforts at peacemaking today may validly be included.

H) BLESSED ARE THE PERSECUTED

Matthew devotes three verses to the congratulation of the persecuted—his special eighth beatitude (v 10) and his version of the fourth Q-beatitude (vv 11-12).

In our initial look at the beatitudes common to Matthew and Luke in part one of this study, we noted that Matthew chooses to underscore the more generalized rejection of persecution rather than formal ostracism. The threefold use of *diōkō* ("I persecute") in vv 10-12 appears to be his work inasmuch as using key words in clusters of three is a favorite rhetorical device for the First Evangelist and persecution is one of his key motifs.[48]

As regards Matthew's special eighth beatitude (v 10), there is a growing consensus that Matthew created this beatitude by putting the sentiment of the last Q-beatitude in the third-person form of his seven other beatitudes. His purpose: to round off the set in a way that echoed the first beatitude ("for theirs is the kingdom of heaven") and the fourth (the motif of righteousness). Moreover, as Guelich observes[49] the subject of the eighth beatitude ("those who are persecuted for righteous-

---

the city was stirred [*eseisthē*]"—with the earthquake image used metaphorically here. The use of the same language on the occasion of the death (27:51-54) and the resurrection (28:2-4) shows that what apocalyptic thinking conceived as the end of "the present age" and the start of "the age to come" was already beginning to happen in the death and resurrection of Jesus.

[48] Matthew will use *diōkō* in three other key places; 5:44 ("pray for those who *persecute* you"), 10:23 ("when they persecute you in one town, flee to the next"), and 23:34, where Christian missionaries are aligned with the prophets of old. For a thorough and balanced study of this motif, see Douglas R. A. Hare, *The Theme of Jewish Persecution of Christians in the Gospel According to St Matthew* (SNTSMS 6; Cambridge: University Press, 1967). Hare finds that Matthew interprets *diōkō* as signifying "those hostile activities which drive Christian missionaries out of a community" (p. 119).

[49] *Sermon*, 93.

ness' sake") is synonymous with the subject of the first ("the poor in spirit"). In naming the subject of the eighth beatitude, Matthew uses a telling grammatical form of *diōkō*: *dediōgmenoi*, the perfect participle passive, which indicates a condition resulting from a past action. *Dediōgmenoi* might be more literally translated, "those who have been persecuted." This suggests that Matthew is addressing a community that has already experienced the persecution in question. The verbs in the following Q-beatitude, however, are in the aorist subjunctive, which means that *future* persecution is in view in these verses. When, then, Matthew integrates his eighth with Q's fourth beatitude, it becomes obvious that he has in mind a community which *has* experienced (v 10) and probably *will* experience (vv 11-12) persecution.

Does the rest of the First Gospel indicate more precisely what kind of persecution Matthew has in mind? This gospel treats of persecution chiefly in two other places, in the middle of the Mission Discourse (10:16-33) and in the seventh woe against the scribes and Pharisees (23:29-36). In his meticulous study of Matthew's redaction in these passages, D. Hare finds that they refer to the informal Jewish rejection and occasional harassment of Jewish Christian missionaries (not formal persecution of rank and file Christians) and that the passages reflect the situation of increased hardening between church and synagogue, when the mission to Israel was seen as a failed enterprise and the church understood itself as a community (of Jews and gentiles) who *replaced* Israel, and whose mission was now directed mainly to the gentiles. Consequently, Hare understands Matthew's version of the Q-beatitude on persecution as applying "primarily to Christian prophets in their mission to unbelieving Israel."[50]

This interpretation would seem to make the beatitude a mere relic, referring to past hostilities. Our study of the audience of the Sermon, however, suggests otherwise. The Sermon is addressed to all those who respond to the invitation of Jesus and thereby become the true messianic Israel. They are assured in the eighth and ninth beatitudes that those who are

---

[50]Hare, *Jewish Persecution*, 121.

persecuted because of their relationship to Jesus are blessed. Matthew's insertion of a word reserved by him for the treatment accorded missionaries by unbelieving Jews, *diōxōsin*, "indicates that the hostile activities mentioned in this beatitude are for him not speculative possibilities but matters of historical experience drawn from the mission to Israel."[51] What has been the lot of the early missionaries to scattered Israel, can, in analogous ways, also be the lot of any and all followers of the rejected Prophet who is also the Son of God.

Regarding this motif of the disciples sharing the lot of the rejected prophets of old, is this simply a tradition inherited from Q or does it also represent a concerted interest of Matthew? We saw that Luke had his way of portraying Jesus and the disciples as the Prophet and his successors. Matthew does this too, in a number of ways. We earlier observed the parallel between the prophetic roles of Jesus and John the Baptist in Mt 1-4. The evangelist continues to ascribe prophetic characteristics to Jesus in subsequent chapters. (1) If Luke evokes the image of the prophet of Yahweh in Is 61 to characterize Jesus, Matthew quotes Is 42:1-4 (Mt 12:18-21). (2) Matthew, alone among the evangelists, associates Jesus with the prophet Jeremiah (the rejected prophet par excellence) in the survey of popular opinion about the Son of man's identity (Mt 16:14), and he alludes to that prophet two other times (2:17 and 27:9). (3) Matthew underscores this prophetic identity of Jesus twice in the episodes beginning the final conflict in Jerusalem: on the occasion of Jesus' entry into Jerusalem, when "all the city" asks, "Who is this?," the crowds answer, "This is the prophet Jesus from Nazareth of Galilee" (21:11). And when the chief priests and the Pharisees try to arrest Jesus after the telling of the parable of The Wicked Vinedressers, "they feared the multitudes, because they held him to be a prophet" (21:46).

Similarly, Matthew has his own way of portraying the disciples as prophets: (1) Towards the end of the speech following the commissioning of the Twelve, the First Evangelist has: "He who receives a prophet because he is a prophet shall

---

[51] Ibid.

receive a prophet's reward" (10:41), and the previous verse makes it clear that all disciples are indicated here ("he who receives you receives me"). (2) Matthew transmits *with elaboration* the Q saying that places Christian prophets in the line of the rejected prophets of old (Mt 23:34-36). (3) In his version of the parable of The Great Banquet, Matthew seems to indicate the continuity between the prophets of the old dispensation with those of the new in the added details of a second group of messengers preceding the doom of Jerusalem (22:1-7).[52]

Matthew's eighth and ninth beatitudes, then, comprise the perfect climax to the entire set. As we have already noted, the eighth beatitude picks up the language of the first and the fourth. It does a variation on the righteousness motif of the fourth by moving from the theme of righteousness as divine gift to the theme of righteousness as human task. By associating the addressees explicitly with the person of Jesus ("on my account"), the ninth beatitude expresses the grounds for congratulation: as followers of Jesus, they are already among the healed and empowered of messianic Israel. Sharing in Jesus' lot can only lead to sharing in his vindication. The promises of both the eighth and ninth macarisms ("theirs *is* the kingdom of heaven" and "your reward is great *in heaven*") embrace the full time focus of the whole: the apocalyptic blessing is grounded in a blessing already experienced through contact with the kingdom available through union with the risen Son of God. The shift from the third-person mode of the first eight beatitudes to the second-person mode ("Blessed are you") facilitates the transition to the body of the Sermon, especially the six antitheses, which climax in a challenge to "love your enemies and pray for those who persecute you" (5:44).

---

[52]Ibid., 121-122.

Afterword

We have taken some care to put the beatitudes back into context in order to hear them in their gospel settings as told by Luke and Matthew. This brief study is just a beginning, but even as a beginning it would not be complete without reflecting on some of what we have learned.

As a professional student and teacher of the Bible, I have been continually startled by a paradox: the more I attend to the differences among the the gospels—differences in structure, thematic interest, style, implied community settings—the more I have been impressed by the way those separate gospels witness to a common tradition and a shared religious experience. Matthew's and Luke's distinctive transmissions of the beatitudes present a stunning illustration of that paradox. Each, in his own "voice" and from his own angle, has presented what we can recognize to be the same speaker, audience, and message. Hearing it from *two* witnesses helps us realize the integrity of their testimony.

The speaker

Both evangelists take care to present Jesus speaking the beatitudes as the end-time Prophet announcing to Israel the imminence of the long-awaited kingdom of God. Luke is the more explicit in his development of this motif. He alludes directly to the prophetic figure of Is 61, heightening the image of the Prophet-like-Moses calling others to share in his prophetic mission, a reality which Luke elaborates in his second volume, Acts. Like Moses, the Lucan Jesus mediates the divine message at the foot of a mountain, recalling Sinai.

Matthew ratifies that interpretation of prophet-and-his people, but he chooses to subordinate it to the picture of the kingly and obedient Son of God calling others to the joy and challenge of sharing, women and men alike, in his "sonship" and "inheritance." As the one who fulfills the end-time expectations for a new David, the Matthean Jesus presides from a mountain whose context suggests end-time Zion.

The audience

In both gospels the audience is, at bottom, the same. The Prophet addresses the end-time gathering of all Israel, a people who have been healed of their infirmities through their contact with Jesus. In Matthew, the beatitudes are taught to the disciples in the hearing of "the crowds." It becomes clear in the remainder of the story that those who accept the good news of the kingdom move from the mere astonishment of the crowds and begin to live with the understanding of disciples. As the new people of God, they inherit the kingdom meant for but lost by the old Israel. In Luke, the plenary gathering is called "the people" and the beatitudes are told especially to the disciples in the hearing of the people. The remainder of Luke's two-volume account makes it clear that those who truly "hear" the Prophet do not become a *new* Israel but show themselves, Jew and gentile alike, to be the *true* people of God and heirs of the promises to Israel. Matthew stresses the break between Israel and its replacement. Luke underscores the continuity.

Although commentators often insist that Luke's "poor" is a more concrete and socio-economic reference than Matthew's "poor in spirit," our examination suggests that the rootedness of both expressions in Isaiah shows the referent to be the same, the poor in Isaiah's sense, those who know their need for God. One can easily imagine Luke approving of Matthew's rendering of the tradition.

In both settings, it is a community that is addressed. Obviously, the response (or resistance) to the words of Jesus is always an act of individual freedom, but the gospel settings remind us that the blessing and challenge of the beatitudes (as well as the Sermon they introduce) have always been the religious experience and mission of a community, a church. One needs to move beyond the individualism of the prevailing culture of the North Atlantic in order to know and live the blessing of the beatitudes. One becomes subject to the congratulations of the beatitudes only by entering the healing environment of a believing community. That is what the church and its sacraments have always been about.

The message.

Both evangelists are faithful to the essence of the message of the Q-beatitudes: the good news of God's long-awaited salvation is now mediated through the person of his Son, Jesus, the Christ. Those poor enough to know their need for this new offer of life are congratulated. To spell out some of the implications of this good news, Matthew and Luke each recast it in a distinctive "package."

Luke underscores the prophetic challenge to decision by setting up a contrast between the congratulations to the poor and the woes to the rich. This is in character with the whole rest of his gospel, which introduces Jesus as "set for the fall and rise of many in Israel ... a sign of contradiction" (Lk 2:34) and climaxes with the death of Jesus between one man who reviles him and another who seeks and finds the kingdom (Lk 22:39-43). The choice is still available to contemporary readers.

Where Luke heightens the alternative options, Matthew stresses the disposition and behavior of the subjects of the congratulation. Elaborating the Q-beatitudes by aligning them with Is 61, enriched by other parts of the prophets and the psalms, Matthew spells out the implications of receiving and implementing the good news.

The time.

Both evangelists make sure their readers hear the beatitudes as spoken within the unfolding of the inauguration of the end-time. For both authors, telling about Jesus in the format of the story of his earthly ministry is simply a way of spelling out the significance of that brief public life as it relates to the Christian communities after the resurrection and the outpouring of the Holy Spirit. Thus, both evangelists can speak of Jesus' speaking the great Sermon as a once-upon-a-time teaching to a Palestinian crowd and (at the same time) present that scenario as a kind of "transparency" which projects the reality of the post-Easter church consoled and challenged by its Risen Lord.

Both evangelists retain the tension of the "already/not yet." The Reign of God is indeed a present reality for those poor enough and child-like enough to receive and share it. At the same time, the full enjoyment of the kingdom remains a future blessing.

Discipleship.

The community which gathered the Q sayings already had made the connection between the congratulations of the poor and those who are hated and reviled on account of the Son of man. Matthew and Luke then elaborate that "cost of discipleship" in their respective gospels. For both, following the prophet means joining Jesus in the long tradition of messengers of God who were rejected by men but vindicated by God. Both acknowledge that following the Prophet who is also more than a prophet, indeed the Son of God, means sharing in the power of his resurrection, especially in mission.

Prophecies or commandments?

People struggling to interpret the beatitudes sometimes ask that question. Does the emphasis fall on the prophetic promises, or is the stress on the description of the subjects (i.e. having the effect of commandments calling for the attitudes and actions implied—being poor in spirit, acting mercifully, making peace, etc.)? Phrased this way, the question poses a false set of alternatives. It is not a matter of *either* (a) prophecy about the future *or* (b) exhortation in the present. It is rather both (a) and (b), and more: apocaylptic prophecy focusing on the present, prophecy whose purpose is to motivate action.

As reflected in the Q-versions, Jesus used the familiar beatitude form to give an apocaylptic message: the kingdom of God is at hand. Matthew and Luke elaborate that primary meaning in the light of Easter by the christologies of their early chapters (the Anointed Son of God and long-awaited Prophet-like-Moses says these things). But they elaborate the beatitudes in function of the *second* part of the traditional summary of Jesus' preaching: *metanoeite* ("repent!" ... "have a change of heart!"). Because of what God has done for us by offering his saving strength in Jesus, choose to be poor and meek, hunger for justice, be merciful, be pure of heart, make peace, risk rejection by identifying with the Son of man.

To use the language of a later theology, in their transmission of the beatitudes, both evangelists reflect the "theology of grace" we associate with St. Paul. Like Paul, Matthew and Luke recognize that the Christian moral life is a matter of "becoming who you are." God takes the initiative by creating community through faith in the revelation that is Jesus. Christian life is a response to that initiative. The gift precedes the task. That is how congratulation can become exhortation without being reduced to some kind of moralism or Pelagianism. As different as their styles of communication may be, Matthew, Luke and Paul are alike in recognizing this.

Recovering the biblical roots of the beatitudes helps us see that what is at stake is something much larger than the affirmation of one economic class over another, or a naive promise of real estate to the nonviolent, or a source of maxims for contemporary peace and justice movements. At the same time, retrieving the gospel context of these sayings helps us recognize that living out the implications of the beatitudes is indeed a radical call to action. Those who identify themselves with the audience of Jesus' great sermon—and Luke and Matthew both mean this audience to be the church—will center their lives on the Creator, recognize the idolatrous pull of wealth and power, struggle against the obscenities of the arms race and legalized abortion, and work strenuously for a more just participation by all in the gifts of the earth. The gift that is the kingdom of God implies such tasks.

The beatitudes stood at the heart of Jesus' preaching. Matthew and Luke passed them on with artistry and pastoral care. Those evangelists remain our best interpreters of the meaning of Jesus' sayings for the post-Easter church.

Suggested Readings

The reader who wants to pursue in greater depth questions of interpretation will find pertinent literature mentioned in the footnotes throughout this book. The list below is for those who want to read one or two books which will further bridge the gap between interpretation and application.

Crosby, Michael H. *Spirituality of the Beatitudes: Matthew's Challenge for First World Christians.* Maryknoll: Orbis,1981. Strong reflections on the implications of the Matthean beatitudes for social justice by an author who has done his exegetical homework.

Galilea, Segundo *The Beatitudes: To Evangelize as Jesus Did.* Maryknoll, NY: Orbis, 1984. Pastoral reflections by a Chilean priest. A good example of the urgency which the experience of the Latin American brings to the beatitudes.

Guelich, Robert A. *The Sermon on the Mount: A Foundation for Understanding* . Waco, TX: Word Books, 1982. The single most helpful contemporary commentary on the Sermon on the Mount. The first 174 pages are devoted to the beatitudes and their setting in Matthew's Gospel, with well developed comparisons to the Lucan parallels and some pastoral asides.

Johnson, Luke T. *Some Hard Blessings: Meditations on the Beatitudes in Matthew.* Allen, TX: Argus, 1982. The edited transcription of retreat talks by a prominent NT scholar.

Lambrecht, Jan, S.J. *The Sermon on the Mount: Proclamation and Exhortation.* Good News Studies 14: Wilmington, DE: Michael Glazier, 1985. An excellent discussion on the Sermon with 35 pages devoted to the beatitudes.

Lapide, Pinchas *The Sermon on the Mount: Utopia or Program for Action?* Maryknoll: Orbis, 1986. The reflection of a Jewish scholar on Matthew 5, with ten pages devoted to the beatitudes. A stunning affirmation of the Jewishness of Jesus by an author who, though he does not accept Jesus as the Messiah, sees him as the best rabbi to interpret the Law of Moses for our times.

Metz, Johannes B. *Poverty of Spirit.* New York: Newman, 1968. This small, 50-page volume is already a classic of contemporary spiritual reading.

Tugwell, Simon *The Beatitudes: Soundings in Christian Traditions.* Springfield, IL: Templegate, 1980. Powerful personal reflections drawing upon the fathers and mothers of the church, ancient and modern.

Index of Scripture References
Old Testament

Exodus
4:22   28, 70
8:19   42
16   53
22:27   96
34:6-7   96, 97

Numbers
12:3   88
14   53

Deuteronomy
4:1   88
7:15   74

2 Samuel
5:6-12   90-91, 105

Psalms
1   10
2:6   72, 76
2:7   27, 70
24:3-6   99-100
32:1-2   9
34   50-51
34:6-10   46
37:11   87-89
85:15   97
102:8   97
112   10
118:22   91
127:5   10
127:1-5   10
144:8   97
144:12-15   10
146:5-7   46

Proverbs
10:10   102

Sirach
25:7-11   10

Isaiah
2:1-4   76, 102, 103
5:8-23   51
6   100
9:1-2   73, 77
25:6   24
26:6   46

29:18-19   22, 42
35:5-6   22, 42
40:9   33
40:28-30   46
42:1   28, 30
42:1-2   91
42:1-4   105, 108
42:6   30
44-66   45
49:6   30, 59
49:9   32
49:10   46
52:7   32, 33
55:1-3   46
55:13   24
56:7-8   76
58:6   25, 31, 64
58:7   64
60:1-4   76
60:6   32
60:20   84
60:21   89
61   34, 36, 45, 50, 57, 60, 64, 79, 80, 84, 87, 92, 108, 110, 112
61:1-2   31, 32, 33, 42, 84
61:1-7   23, 25, 26
61:3   92
61:6   24, 32
61:7   89
61:8   92-93
62:11   90
65:13-14   24
66:10-11   84-85

Jeremiah
31:12   76
31:23   76

Daniel
7:13, 21   42
8:19   42
9:21ff   42
12:12-13   11

Hosea
6:6   98, 99, 100
11:1   28, 70, 103

Zechariah
9:9-10   90-91, 105

Intertestamental Literature

1QM
14:7   80

4QpPs37   88

4QMelch   24

New Testament

Matthew
1:18   70
1:20   70
1:21   69, 77
2:1-12   77
2:13-23   70
2:15   70, 103
2:17   108
3:2   72, 83
3:13-17   70-72, 91, 103
3:15   94, 95
4:3   103
4:6   103
4:8-10   91
4:12   73
4:15-16   73, 77
4:17   75, 83
4:18-20   78
4:23   74, 77
4:25   75, 78
5:1-2   77, 78
5:3   80, 81, 86
5:3-12   13f., 17
5:4   86-87
5:5   86-92
5:6   92-96
5:8   80, 99-101
5:9   102-106
5:10-12   106-109

5:10	95	19:23-24	81, 82, 83	1:35	36
5:11	95	20:21	83	1:45-55	66-67
5:11-12	15, 83	20:30-31	98	1:47	29
5:13-14	75, 77, 78	21:5	90, 91	1:53-55	39
5:20	93, 95	21:11	108	1:67	39
5:21-48	93, 101	21:28-31	94	1:68	38
5:44	106, 109	21:31	82, 83, 84	1:69	29
5:48	97	21:32	94, 95	1:75	93
6:1	93, 95	21:33-43	91	1:76	30
6:10	82	21:43	82	1:77	38
6:14-15	97	21:41	91	1:80	39
6:16-18	86	21:46	108	2:4	29
6:33	94	22:1-14	86, 109	2:10	33, 38, 39
7:1-2	97	23	53	2:11	29, 30
7:21	83, 93	23:23	99	2:25	39, 42
7:28-29	74, 75	23:25-26	54	2:26	30
8:21-22	78	23:24-36	107, 109	2:31	38
8:1	78	23:34	95, 106	2:32	27, 38, 39,
9:9	78	25:1-2	86		60
9:13	98, 100	25:31-46	99	2:34	39, 112
9:14-17	85	25:34	83, 89	2:35	42
9:15	85	26:9	81	2:49	32
9:27	98	26:11	81	3:1-3	30
9:35	74	26:28	69	3:10	46
10:1	78	27:9	108	3:15	30, 38
10:7	83	27:51-54	106	3:18	33, 38
10:23	95, 106	27:57	81	3:21-22	34, 38
10:41	109	28:2-4	106	3:21-4:44	35
11:4-6	22, 24	28:16-20	72, 105	3:23-38	28
11:5	81	28:20	69	3:31	29
11:12	83			4:1-13	28
11:15	32	**Mark**		4:14	36
11:16-19	85	1:15	73	4:16-30	34
11:29	80, 91	1:16-20	35	4:21	42
12:1	98	1:31	32	4:31-41	34
12:7	98, 100	1:36	32	4:16-44	31, 38
12:13-21	104-105	2:18-22	85	4:18-19	25, 26, 33,
12:18-21	108	3:7-12	37		50
12:28	22, 24, 42.	3:13-19	37, 74	4:31-32	31
	82, 83, 91	6:3	47	4:36	31, 36
13:15-23	101	6:6-13	74	4:39	32
13:44-45	83	7:21-22	101	4:41	30
13:55	47	10:21	97	4:42-43	32, 33, 34,
14:20	95				43
15:22	98	**Luke**		5:2	53
15:29-31	95	1-2	27	5:1-6:19	35
15:33	95	1:7	46	5:8-23	51
15:37	95	1:10	38	5:13	35
16:14	108	1:15	30	5:16	36
17:15	98	1:17	30, 38	5:17	40, 53
18:3	83	1:21	38	5:17-6:11	35
18:20	69	1:19	33	5:21	53
18:23-35	97-98	1:25	46	5:26	42
19:14	83	1:27	29	5:29-32	65
19:21	81, 97	1:32	27, 29	5:30	53
		1:33	39		

6:2	53	14:1	46	**Acts**	
6:7	53, 56	14:12	51	2:17	43
6:12-16	39	14:13, 21	45	2:29-21	27
6:17-20	37-41, 50	14:14	61, 64	2:30-36	29, 43
6:20	56	14:15	43	3	46
6:20b-26	13f., 17	14:15-24	61-62	3:22-23	49
6:21	63	15:1-8	65	3:24	43
6:22-23	15	15:16	63	4:34-35	46
6:24-26	55, 65	16	55-56	5:31	29
6:29-30	46	16:1	51	5:41-42	60
6:34-35	97	16:13	63	5:43-48	103-104
6:36	97	16:14	52	6:1-6	46
6:46	58	16:16	43	8:4	61
7:1	38, 40	16:19	51	8:12	61
7:11-12	46	16:19-31	63-65	8:25	61
7:16	48	16:20	44-51	8:35	61
7:17	38	16:22	44, 51	10:36-38	34
7:19	42	17:20	42	11:20	61
7:22-23	22, 26, 50	18	58	13:1	59
7:26	30	18:1-8	46	13:23	29
7:29-30	53	18:9	56	13:32	61
7:36-50	53	18:15-17	47, 66	13:46-47	59
8:1	43	18:22	44	14:7	61
8:3	48	18:24-25	52	14:15	61
8:10	43	18:25	51, 65	14:21	61
8:12-18	41	18:33	51	15:16-18	43, 63
8:28	28	18:35-40	46	15:32	59
9	47	18:38-39	29	15:35	61
9:2-11	40, 43	19:1	51	16:10	61
9:17	63	19:1-10	65-66	17:18	61
9:22	32	19:5, 9	42	21:10	59
9:27	43	19:8	44	26:22-23	27, 59
9:35	28	19:11	43		
9:51-		19:11-27	66	**Romans**	
19:27	17	19:37	39	4	9
9:57	47	19:39	57	8:16	103
10	47	20:20	56	8:21	103
10:9	40, 43	20:41f.,			
11:2	43	44	29	**Philippians**	
11:20	22, 42, 43	21:1-3	42, 52	2:15	103
11:27-28	1, 66-67	21:3	44		
11:37-52	53, 54	21:31	43	**Hebrews**	
11:42	54, 99	22:29-30	43	2:17	96
11:47-48	60	22:39-43	112		
11:53-54	54	22:70	29	**James**	
12:1	54	23:5	38	1:12	11
12:13-21	62-63	23:43	42		
12:16	51, 65	24:19	49	**1 Peter**	
12:31	43			3:14	59
13:10-17	63	**John**		4:13-14	59
13:28-29	43, 60	1:12	103		
		11:52	103	**1 John**	
				3:1, 2, 10	103
				5:2	103

Author Index

Achtemeier, E. 24, 25
Alonso-Schoekel, L. 87
Bailey, K. 62, 63
Bammel, E. 64
Barre, M. 100
Batdorf, I. 88
Baumbach, G. 52
Beasley-Murray, G. 14
Brown, R. 42, 70
Brueggemann, W. 91
Cazelles, H. 3
Chilton, B. 33, 34
Clifford, R. 24
Cope, O. L. 98
Donaldson, T. 72, 76, 77, 95
Dupont, J. 3, 14, 80, 93, 95, 96, 99
Farris, S. 30, 67
Fitzmyer, J. 14, 28, 93, 95
Foerster, W. 88, 102
Guelich, R. 3, 14, 78, 81, 93, 95, 99
Hamm, D. 63, 66
Hare, D. 106-109
Hauck, F. 3, 9, 44

Horgan, M. 88
Janzen, W. 3, 8, 12
Jervell, J. 43
Johnson, E. 89
Koch, K. 11
Lambrecht, J. 3, 19, 93, 95
Lohfink, G. 74, 75
Marshall, I. 21, 25
McEleney, N. 3, 14
Mealand, D. 49
Meier, J. 86, 105
Metzger, B. 12
Moxnes, H. 52
Neyrey, J. 28
Pamment, M. 82
Perrin, N. 21
Reumann, J. 93, 95
Schrenk, G. 93
Schweizer, E. 105
Seccombe, D. 45
Sloan, R. 24
Suggs, M. 89
Traub, H. 82